WHAT A CARRY ON

The Official Story of the Carry On Film Series

WHAT A CARRY ON

The Official Story of the Carry On Film Series

Introduction by Peter Rogers
Compiled by
Sally Hibbin and Nina Hibbin

HAMLYN

Below: Sir Sidney and Lady Ruff-Diamond (Sid James and Joan Sims) uphold the finest traditions of the Raj in *Up The Khyber*.

Below right: itching powder creates havoc in the headmaster's study in *Teacher*. Suffering here are (left to right) Charles Hawtrey, Hattie Jacques and Kenneth Williams.

Published in 1988
by The Hamlyn Publishing Group Limited
a division of The Octopus Publishing Group,
Michelin House, 81 Fulham Road, London SW3 6RB

ISBN 0 600 55819 3

Printed in Italy

Contents

Right: (from left to right) Carry On producer Peter Rogers signs the deal with Nat Cohen and Stuart Levy of Anglo-Amalgamated for the third Carry On in the series, *Carry On Teacher*. By now, everyone knew that they had a winning formula but did they know how long it would Carry On?

Below: originally titled *Call Me a Cab*, it was clear from the start that this would be another Carry On. Its title changed again from *Taxi* to *Cabby* to become the fourth in the highly successful series.

Introduction

by Peter Rogers

Comedy is not funny. At least, that is what Gerald Thomas and I discovered when we graduated – or deteriorated, according to taste – from films like *Time Lock*, which was about a little boy locked in a security vault, and Francis Durbridge thrillers, to what became known as the Carry On series. Gerald and I have been together for a long time. We started as friends and ended up as partners and, to date, have made more than 50 films together and no end of TV series, earning the nickname Rogers & Thomastein.

Then a script called *The Bull Boys*, written by R. F. Delderfield, landed on my desk. It was a love story about two ballet dancers, one of whom was caught up in the web, applicable at that time, of conscription. The script had been offered to a number of distributors and had been turned down. (If you have a few hours to spare, I'll tell you about the difference between distributors and producers. In a nutshell, distributors think they know all about production, and producers think they know all about distribution. Actually, distributors finance producers.)

I realized that there was only one thing to do with a drama nobody wants – make it funny. How to make it funny?

The first person I approached was Eric Sykes, whose comedy writing I had always admired. I caught him on a bad day. He'd just had a nasty experience with a nasty producer who owed him money and he told me in no uncertain terms what I could do with my script. In the same building were Spike Milligan, Alan Simpson, Ray Galton, John Antrobus and a few more. It was a kind of Dr Barnado's with typewriters run by a sympathetic agent-cum-matron named Beryl Vertue. The inmate who volunteered to turn *The Bull Boys* into a comedy was John Antrobus. He changed it into a very funny script, but it lacked logic and, rightly or wrongly, I feel that audiences like to believe in their comedy, even to the point of the odd tug at the heartstrings. (John Antrobus has done a lot of work for me and Gerald since those days.)

So far, no luck. Then, like a fool, I realized that I had a writer under contract who was clocking up 'idle time'. I asked him if he'd like to try his hand at a comedy, something he hadn't done before. Norman Hudis was a serious writer. By that I mean he wrote serious subjects. In the 1930s he had fought Mosley's Blackshirts in the Dalston High Street demonstrations, and had started in the film business as a publicist. But a writer is a writer is a writer, and he turned *The Bull Boys* into the comedy I envisaged – combining laughter and tears. Little did I realise that we would be crying all the way to the bank.

But I'm going too fast.

Having moulded *The Bull Boys* to my liking, I went to a distribution company by the name of Anglo Amalgamated who hitherto had bought foreign films and American films and released them through the Associated British (ABC) circuit. The gentleman I saw was Stuart Levy, a lovely man, small, round and quite bald. At first sight he appeared to have more skin than he was entitled to but he had a lovely smile and, most important, a sense of humour. He became a dear friend and when he died I thought the bottom had fallen out of my film world. He liked the script and wanted me to make the film. He introduced me to his partner, Nat Cohen, who, although he hadn't read the script, liked the idea of it as recited by Stuart and obviously concurred with anything Stuart wanted. Later I discovered that their relationship was very much like mine with Gerald.

The one thing Stuart didn't like was the title. He wanted it changed to *Carry On Sergeant*. At that time there was a very successful film called *Carry On Admiral* going the rounds. Distributors are a bit like sheep, for whom there is only one gap in the hedge, and Stuart thought another comedy with a similar title would be equally successful. I wondered about the title clash but he assured me it would be no problem. That came later.

To direct the film I went to Val Guest, who had directed *Carry On Admiral*. He didn't want to do it. (Or he didn't want to do it for the money I offered.) Then for a second time fate took a hand, waking me up with a kick in the backside. I had a director under contract who, like Norman Hudis, had never tackled comedy. But a director is a director is a director. That director was Gerald Thomas. We had made several films together and were close friends. We'd also had many laughs together, so why not try to put a few on celluloid?

And so Gerald Thomas and I embarked upon the production of the first Carry On, blithely unaware that it was the first of anything. We thought it was just another film. But it was our first comedy, so we tackled it as professionally and as economically as we knew how. Our approach to comedy was to avoid being consciously funny.

If an actor had a funny line, or did anything funny, he should be unaware of it. (I remember that in the next film, *Carry On Nurse*, one of the nurses laughed as she delivered her line. We had to shoot it again.)

Nobody had any idea that *Carry On Sergeant* would take off as it did. Conscription was old hat at the time but it made no difference. Even at the plush charity premiere of *The Devil's Disciple*, it struck a chord. There is a scene in the Laurence Olivier epic when one of the Redcoat Officers turns to his NCO and says 'Carry on, Sergeant'. The whole audience roared with laughter. And at the last night of the Proms that year, when Sir Malcolm Sargent was conducting, many of the promenaders were waving huge banners with the legend, 'Carry on Sargent'. The phrase became so popular that you'd almost think we had invented the two words and that they had never been part of the English language until the film came along.

As a producer, I was still buying other subjects and commissioning writers to present me with screenplays, but whenever I tried to interest Stuart Levy in them he'd say, 'Oh, no. Give us another Carry On'. So I put the other subjects aside and contented myself with turning out Carry Ons or comedies which fitted into the Carry On pattern.

Gerald Thomas and I have always been so attuned to the work that we are almost carbon copies of each other. We have identical reactions to a script and each scene of a script and when we sit in the viewing theatre running the completed film (known as the Assembly), we nudge each other when we think a cut is necessary. Usually our nudges are simultaneous. The same thing happens when we run the Rough Cut (the next stage after the Assembly) and the Fine Cut (the next stage after the Rough Cut). It is a rapport which is probably unique in the business. Journalists have been known to say that, having interviewed each of us separately, we recite the same statements.

Naturally we've had some laughs together. For example, on the first day of shooting, I always buy a jar of caviar to share with Gerald in my office – a caravan on the set. On one occasion I couldn't open the jar. I wrestled with it, but it would not budge. With a cry of 'Oh, bugger it!', I hurled the jar and its expensive contents at the wall of the caravan. That opened it alright, and Gerald and I spent the next five minutes on our hands and knees scooping the caviar off the carpet and spreading it on our toast.

Some critics call the Carry Ons the most successful British film series of all time. Other critics look down their noses at them and consider them vulgar and crude. But filmgoers embraced them from the start, and this was at a time when television was luring audiences away from the cinema. The Carry Ons have always been in the charts – the ultimate barometer of public opinion. They have always been in the top ten. The sequel to *Carry On Sergeant*, *Carry On Nurse*, shot to the top of the charts. It was also a big hit in America, where *Carry On Sergeant* had failed, principally because Americans have never really been aware that we have an army. *Carry On Nurse* ran for over two years in the

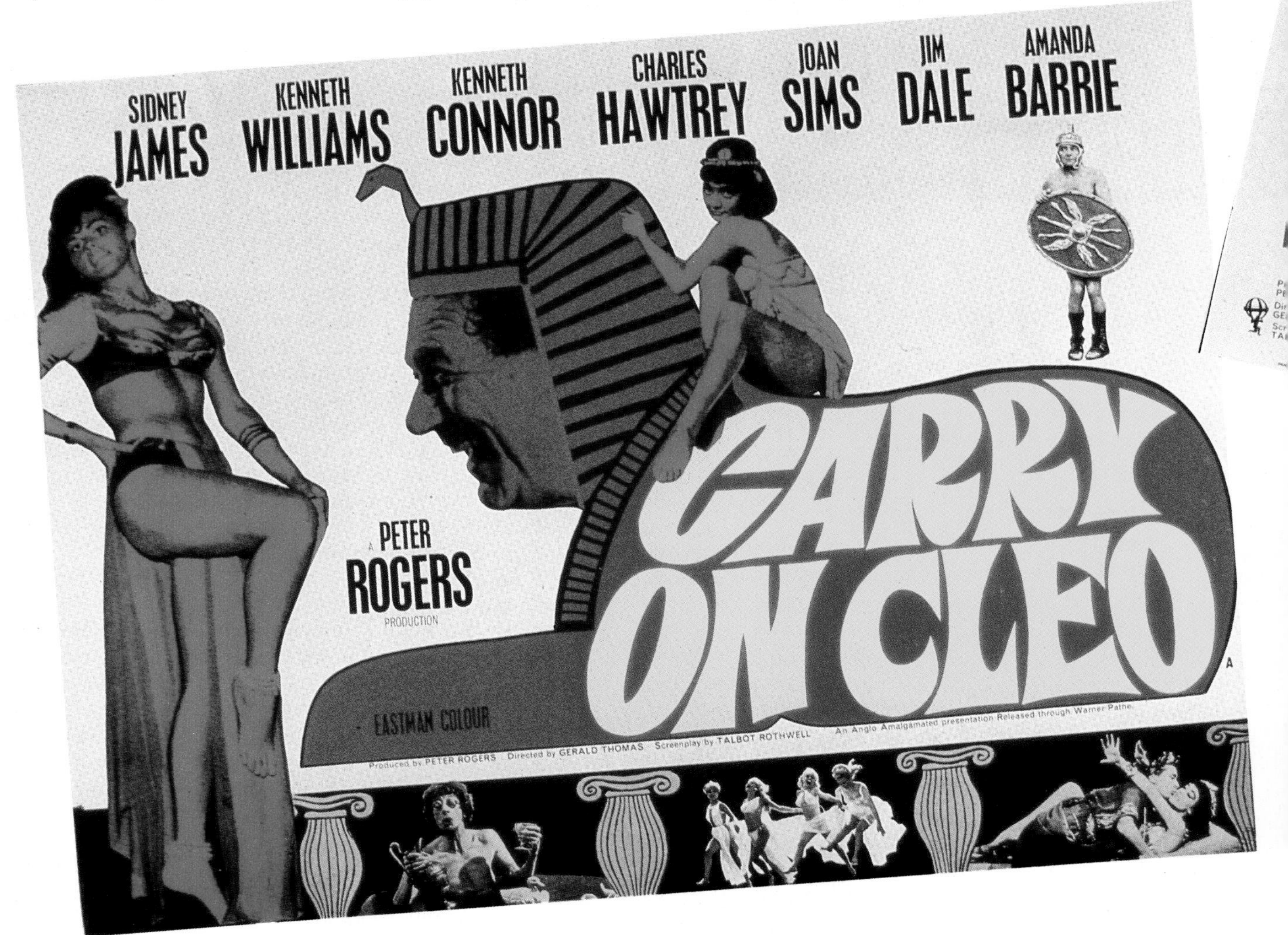

Opposite: while the poster for *Cleo* evokes the atmosphere of ancient Egypt, the film itself was shot – as always – at Pinewood Studios. Here the team were helped by the sets for *Cleopatra* which had been abandoned at Pinewood when the cast and crew of the disastrous epic decamped for Rome.

Left: *Spying*, a spoof on the popular James Bond films, carries its puns into the poster

Above: Kenneth Williams and Leslie Phillips, still in costume as two of the latest recruits to the boys in blue, apprehend director Gerald Thomas on the set of *Constable*, the second in the series. The Carry Ons are legendary for their relaxed atmosphere on the set and the occasional spot of high jinks from the cast.

States, and a million plastic daffodils were produced to publicise its success. And so on and so on, as the conductor says at the end of Strauss's 'Perpetuum Mobile'. The films have spanned generations, particularly since they have been repeated so often on television and are now available on video.

Everybody has their favourite Carry On and each new release is often greeted by some of the fans with the reaction that 'It's not as good as the last one'. My own favourite is *Carry On Up The Khyber*. Gerald's is *Carry On Camping*.

Gerald has directed them all and we've had surprisingly few writers. You could almost say that Norman Hudis and Talbot Rothwell wrote them all between them, Talbot Rothwell taking over when Norman Hudis decided to go to America. And Eric Rogers (no relation) has written the music for all but one or two. Every film in the series has been shot at Pinewood – on the stages, on the back lot, in the garden, in the paddock, in the car park, in the board room, in the restaurant, and in the bar. For locations, Windsor has stood in for London for more times than I care to remember. Maidenhead Town Hall has been a hospital on several occasions. For *Carry On Cruising* we never left the stages at all. On a couple of occasions we ventured farther afield to Snowdonia, in Wales, for *Carry On Up The Khyber*; and to Camber Sands, in Sussex, for *Carry On, Follow That Camel*.

When it comes to casting, Gerald and I made it quite clear to every artiste – whatever their status – that the star of the film was the phrase 'Carry On'. Everybody else's name came under the title. We did it this way so that no one could call himself a star and so lord it over the others. Either they accepted that they were part of a team or they weren't in the film. We have never compromised on this principle, and I'm sure, that it has preserved the uniqueness of the Carry Ons. Mind you, artistes being what they are, something akin to spoilt children, it was no rare thing for an artiste's agent to ring me up and complain that so and so was getting more money than his client.

Equally important was our decision not to fall into the trap of recruiting comics – which could have been disastrous – but to attract actors and actresses who could play comedy without trying to be funny. There is a world of difference.

People ask me, 'What is the Carry On formula?' I am not aware that there is one. If there is one essential ingredient it is familiarity. I am convinced that audiences do not like

Above: Sid James gets out his chopper for the poster of *Henry*, a Carry on hysterical historical which took the team back to the English court of Tudor times where King Henry had his well-documented difficulties in deciding which wife he wants at any one time.

Right: (from left to right) Sid James, Barbara Windsor, director Gerald Thomas, Joan Sims and Julian Holloway enjoy a romp between takes in the grounds of Pinewood Studios, the setting for *Henry*.

change; they like the same thing over and over again. It's like being married – and more people stay married than get divorced. If you give the audience what they want, they will remain faithful to you. Our films did not make fun of people in the satirical sense. We didn't lampoon people. Satire is too easy. It's simply another way of being bitchy. Nor were our films ever farcical. The situations created in our films were not impossible. Improbable, yes, but not impossible. We always aimed to show people how funny they could be in a warm, human way. In *Carry on Henry*, when Lord Hampton of Wick bursts in saying, 'Your Majesty, the Queen is in labour', Henry replies, 'Don't worry. They'll never get back!' This is the kind of topical joke that we only occasionally let go by because it wouldn't mean a thing in the rest of the world. The same applies to the situation in *Carry On Up the Khyber*. When Princess Jelhi is worried about her boy friend suffering death from a thousand cuts, the Khasi of Kalabar answers, 'Nonsense. The British are used to cuts.' This got a bit of a laugh because it was non-political, it could apply to anybody at any time. The real laugh – and again non-translatable – was when the Khasi called his daughter Jelhi-baby.

The real humour of the Carry On's has its basis in the seaside picture postcard, the broad music hall joke. I remember on one occasion buying a whole set of seaside picture postcards from the publishers and sending them to the censor as a guide to the kind of humour to expect from us. He never sent them back. The critics who dismiss Carry On humour as old-fashioned do not realize that audiences like to see the laughs coming and to recognize them.

It has been our experience that hospitals and history have always been surefire Carry On subjects. We steer clear of subjects that might coincide with some fatality. We had a script called 'Carry On Smoking' which was about the Fire Brigade. We wouldn't touch it in case some tragic fire took place when the film was on release. The same attitude applied to 'Carry On Flying'.

The script of a Carry On always starts with the title, from which everything else stems. In selling a Carry On subject to a distributor, I rarely need to go beyond the title and a few outrageous names for the characters. The rest is understood, because it is virtually impossible for other people to judge a Carry On simply by what is written on the paper. Sometimes it goes further than that. When we were shooting *Carry On Sergeant*, I sent the rushes up to Anglo Amalgamated for them to see. I did it out of courtesy. After all, they were putting up all the money. I didn't send them for their assessment. For about a week I had worried

telephone calls from them saying it wasn't funny, what did I think I was playing at? After that I sent no more rushes to London. They didn't seem to notice. When they saw the finished film, they laughed their heads off. I never sent them rushes again, but they would sometimes come down to the studio to watch the shooting and seemed to go away happy. Maybe that was because they had been photographed with a pretty starlet.

Carry On scripts were never submitted from outside. It seemed almost impossible for outside writers to envisage the casting or the formula or familiarity. The idea and story line were created by discussion between me, director Gerald Thomas, and the writer. I dreamed up the title and, when working with scriptwriter Norman Hudis, tossed the subject about between us until Norman felt confident enough to go away and write a draft screenplay, which he would submit a few weeks later. Gerald and I read it, discussed it together and then called in Norman for a conference. No conference ever lasted for more than a couple of hours, such was the rapport between us. If any further work was necessary on the script, Gerald used to say to me, 'Looks as if you're going to have a few days at home.' That meant that I would stay at home for a few days licking the script into shape – one of the happiest moments in the production, at least for me, since I started in the business as a script writer and still cannot resist putting my spoke in. I would then submit the final script to Gerald for his approval. After that it became what Gerald called 'The Bible'. Nothing was ever changed after that and if an artiste suggested some change to Gerald, he told them that he knew what he was doing. All done in a friendly way, of course. And now let me say a word about censorship.

Gerald and I have always had a running battle with the censor. During the course of our partnership we have had to deal with several censors. To avoid any libel or slander, I'll call them all The Censor.

When we had to cut one or two gags from *Carry On Sergeant* which were thought unsuitable for family audiences, Anglo suggested that we should put them back once the Censor had seen the cuts. Imagine what would have happened then! The Board of Trade would have banned us from the business. Anglo's idea of negotiation was to lunch the Censor and spend the afternoon taking him round the strip clubs. That may have worked when they were importing their foreign films but I didn't fancy the idea for our comedies. Our tactics were more subtle. Gerald and I always made a point of slipping one or two gags into the films which were calculated to catch The Censor's eye, so that when we went to see him in his office above Soho Square we could bargain – we'll take this out if you'll keep that in. He was always frightened that if Father laughed at a risqué joke, his Son would ask him what he was laughing at and the Father would be too embarrassed to explain. That was the Censor's yardstick. To give him his due, he understood the purpose of our films (even if we didn't) and always said that he thought that they were well made. He said they didn't look cheap – which was a compliment, knowing what they cost and what some critics thought of them. (As far as expenditure was concerned, we never stinted on technicians.) But we had a bit of a barney with the Censor on one particular occasion. We happened to know that he had let by in an American film a similar gag to the one he had cut out of ours. By way of explanation he said, 'Oh, but that was an American film and it cost a lot of money, a good deal more than yours'.

As for the future, more Carry On films will be made as and when time and finance permit. The compilations which appear on your television screens are not made in five minutes. There are miles and miles of film to view and the whole process takes nearly 12 months. Apart from any feature films we also plan a series of what we call television 'Specials' – that is, Carry On films of nearly an hour in length for showing on television.

Fingers crossed.

Peter Rogers

The Making of the Carry Ons

They've been together now for 30 Carry Ons – producer Peter Rogers and director Gerald Thomas – in one of the longest and most profitable creative partnerships in British film history. They are as different as chalk and cheese: Rogers has an air of eccentricity and a colourful turn of phrase combined with shrewd business sense; Thomas is more serene and avuncular, with a manner not unlike the bedside one he would have adopted if he'd finished his medical training.

Between them there is a complex tangle of relatives, all of whom are film-makers. Rogers is married to producer Betty Box, whose numerous films include the popular Doctor series, all of which have been directed by Ralph Thomas, Gerald's older brother. In the Fifties, Gerald worked as an editor in the cutting room with producer Betty Box. Gerald had ambitions to direct and Peter, then a young producer, backed him. Together they make a formidable team whose skills have combined to create a British institution.

It took them a year to set up their first film. *Circus Friends*, written by Peter Rogers, was an amiable adventure story for the Children's Film Foundation, in which a girl rescues a pony destined for the knacker's yard. At Beaconsfield studios they made several pictures together, working on tight schedules and even tighter budgets. They were suspense films rather than comedies, including the highly praised *Time Lock* (1957), written by Arthur Haley, which gave Sean Connery his first speaking role; and *Vicious Circle* (1957), with John Mills in the lead.

Peter Rogers had the rights to R F Delderfield's story, *The Bull Boys*, a straightforward account of a ballet-dancer whose boyfriend is called up on the day they are to be married. Rogers saw its potential for comedy and he tells a possibly apochryphal story of how he found a scriptwriter. He went to Eric Sykes who, feeling sore after a recent hassle in the film industry, told him that all producers were shits and abruptly showed him the door. Then he went to Spike Milligan, who had a revolver on his desk. 'I'm going to shoot my wife', he announced. Rogers advised him that it might be easier to divorce her and went instead to Norman Hudis.

Hudis's script cut out the ballet dancer and concentrated on barrack-room life, whose comic aspects had been popularized by TV's *The Army Game*. Rogers liked it and secured backing from Anglo-Amalgamated. Anglo's boss, Stuart Levy, came up with the title, *Carry On Sergeant*. Halfway through the filming the Anglo chiefs took fright

The Carry On team massed outside of the main fort set for *Follow That Camel*. The eagle-eyed can spot several members of the team resting while the shot is set up. Note, in the background, the sea. This was one of the few occasions when the team left the studio for a more exotic location – the Sussex coast.

Producer Peter Rogers and director Gerald Thomas swap notes on the set of *Follow That Camel*. Note, this time, however, that it looks suspiciously like Pinewood Studios once again.

The mind boggles to think what director Gerald Thomas is doing on the set of *Girls*. In fact, he is giving directions for the scene in which Patsy Rowlands, as the Mayor's wife, is initiated into the ways of Fircombe-on-Sea's women's liberation movement. 'Pass me the candle', says Councillor Prodworthy (June Whitfield) suggestively.

after seeing some of the rushes. They said it was not funny and threatened to withdraw. For Rogers and Thomas, who could see that the jokes were working, the solution was simple. They didn't show Anglo any more rushes until shooting was finished. Their confidence was justified by the results. A low budget film costing £74,000, it took everybody, including Rogers and Thomas, by surprise, when it leapt into third place in the 1958 box office ratings. It cried out for a follow-up. *Carry On Nurse* did even better. It not only topped the box office charts, but also ran for two and a half years in the United States.

One film led to another until it was clear that there was a series. At first there were three Carry Ons per year, then two, and by the Seventies just one. After *Screaming*, Anglo-Amalgamated pulled out. Rogers offers a possible explanation. 'Anglo', he says, 'got the culture bit between their teeth'. Rank took up the option but not, at first, the Carry On title. The next two films, *Don't Lose Your Head* and *Follow That Camel*, were given their Carry On prefix some years later. When Rank pulled out of film production in Britain, Hemdale stepped in and backed *Emmannuelle*. Over the years the films have made a fortune – not only for the distributors but also for Rogers and Thomas, who are both millionaires.

Peter Rogers was born in Rochester, Kent, in 1914. He started his career in journalism, first on a local paper and then in Fleet Street, and tried his hand at writing radio plays for the BBC. He entered the film business as a writer of five-minute religious shorts, called 'Thought for the Week', for J. Arthur Rank. After the war, when he was working as a scriptwriter for Gainsborough Pictures, he teamed up with his future wife, Betty Box, one of Britain's top film producers. They collaborated successfully on a number of productions at the old Islington Studios and later at Gainsborough Studios in Shepherds Bush. Rogers made several children's films, including *The Dog and the Diamond*, which won a Venice Film Festival award in 1953.

Even when the Carry On films became the focal point of Rogers' career, he remained a prolific producer, making well over 100 films, most of them with Thomas as director. He now lives in Beaconsfield and has two other great loves in his life – animals and music; the degree of these two passions is expressed by his determination to leave his considerable fortune to animal charities and the establishment of a music scholarship.

Gerald Thomas was born in 1920 in Hull, Yorkshire. He

was educated at Bristol and London and studied to become a doctor. During the war he served with the Royal Sussex Regiment in Europe and the Middle East. When he was demobilized, he entered the film industry as an assistant editor at Denham Studios and worked on outstanding films like *The October Man* (1947) and Laurence Olivier's *Hamlet* (1948). In 1948 he was given his first assignment as an editor, on *Madness of the Heart*. His associate editor credits are impressive, including *The Third Man* (1949) and *Pandora and the Flying Dutchman* (1950). In his partnership with Peter Rogers he discovered his niche in comedy, but is equally at home in other styles. He lives near Pinewood studios and is a dedicated family man, devoted to his wife Barbara and daughters Sarah, Deborah and Samantha.

As the producer, Rogers is largely concerned with the financial side of the Carry Ons (although he is proud of having contributed to the scripts and has over the years had a guiding influence on the music). He is also the arbiter of the artistic content. All the Carry Ons have been made without a dollar of American money – no mean achievement in an industry which has traditionally relied heavily on American capital. Rogers, who regards himself as a true Brit, revels in the Britishness of his films, has never been to the United States and has no wish to go there. He believes the foundation of the series' success is the fact that 'we never, never, *never* lose sight of the audience'. He argues that his understanding of what makes the Carry Ons tick does not stem from any carefully researched analysis but 'from the navel'.

His navel has not served him badly. The Carry On films have regularly appeared in the top ten lists, and even today their television exposure can beat Coronation Street in the ratings. As Rogers points out, every seven years there is a new generation of youngsters to enjoy them. In addition, they have sold around the world and have all been highly profitable. The country where they are least successful is France. As Rogers dryly observes, 'we talk about it: they do it'. He reckons they have only made a couple of mistakes but he is careful not to name them as they concern casting.

The Carry Ons are low budget films made to the limit of what can be raised by British finance alone, and this shapes both the way they are produced and their style of comedy. Their tight shooting schedules never exceed six weeks. There is no elaborate cosseting of the cast. There are no stars, no massive salaries, no overtime, no big expense accounts and no far-away locations. Much of the films' humour flows from the deliberately make-shift way in which the scenes are often set: the Welsh farm gate which guards the Khyber Pass in *Carry On Up The Khyber*; or the windblown South coast sand dunes along which the desert legionnaires tramp in *Follow That Camel*.

If Rogers is the Barnum of the Carry On circus, Thomas is its ringmaster. 'We've all been at it together for so long', he says, 'that everyone knows everyone else's style and pace. I find myself less and less having to direct. I just crack a whip and everyone goes through their paces'. He ensures that the schedule is maintained by ironing out all the problems in advance and then sticking strictly to what has been planned. Actors can make suggestions and add things during rehearsal, but once shooting begins no ad-libbing is allowed. 'The script is our Bible', Thomas explains, and the cast are chosen for their professionalism and their ability to bring their own style and interpretation to the written words.

The relaxed atmosphere of the Carry On sets is legendary. While other film sets often have a cathedral-like hush, both Rogers and Thomas boast of the happy, easygoing conditions. Thomas is something of a father confessor to his 'family' of 'unruly children', listening to everybody's problems and offering advice. He has a great sense of fun and enjoys playing tricks on his cast – filling Joan Sims' glass with gin instead of water while filming the drunk scene in *Regardless*; or hosing down the beauty contestants in *Girls*, when they were expecting a mild damping from the sprinkler.

'It's fun making them', says Thomas. 'It's not like work, more like a holiday. It's like going back to school and being a headmaster'. Rogers puts it differently. 'I consider myself a servant of the public', he says, 'and I thoroughly enjoy satisfying them. I'm an entertainer'.

It's not all fun and games on the set. Charles Hawtrey is clearly averse to landing in the soup in *Camping* – even if he is being spoonfed by Gerald Thomas. The muddy field in which the action takes place is, of course, not far from Pinewood.

It's lonely at the top. Producer Peter Rogers updates his script in the wilds of the Sussex dunes.

Scriptwriters

Norman Hudis

'It's the thrill of a lifetime', said Hudis when in 1959 he heard that *Carry On Nurse* was the top box-office film of the year. The success of *Sergeant*, number three in the charts the previous year, had also taken him by surprise. He left it to others, he confessed, to find out what makes the box-office tick: He simply regarded the assignment as a chance to prove himself a comedy writer.

Born in 1923, Hudis started his professional life as a trainee reporter on the *Hampstead and Highgate Express*. During the war, as an airman in the Middle East, he wrote for Air Force News. Nursing an early ambition to become a serious playwright, he wrote several dramas including *Here Is the News*. It did not get beyond a try-out at Leatherhead but attracted good reviews and earned him a place at Pinewood as a trainee scriptwriter. After two years, and nothing on the screen, he took the bold step of going freelance. He became a prolific writer of B-movies, sometimes churning out three scripts simultaneously.

It was Carry On's Peter Rogers who gave Hudis his first big break, scripting *The Tommy Steele Story*. This, too, began as a B-movie but was quickly promoted to main feature status. Hudis felt a particular affinity with Steele – they both came from the same Cockney background – and he followed up with another vehicle for the pop star, *The Duke Wore Jeans*, directed by Gerald Thomas.

When Rogers and Thomas were looking for someone to turn R F Delderfield's *The Bull Boys* into a film, Hudis was the natural choice. The success of the film, released as *Carry On Sergeant*, led to his working on five more Carry Ons before he was lured to the United States, where he currently works as a jobbing TV writer.

The six Hudis Carry On scripts differ from the later Talbot Rothwell scripts in their soft-centred approach. Unlike Rothwell's, most of them are tightly plotted with all the ends neatly tied up. They are usually set in establishments or institutions where stern discipline is imposed by uniformed authorities, although it is the underdogs who call the shots. In *Sergeant*, it is not the NCOs who win the day, but the men who finally make the decision to pull together and back them. In *Teacher*, it is the young 'saboteurs', not the staff, who make all the running.

Many of Hudis's scripts have an insider feel about them. For *Sergeant*, he drew on his own experiences in the services. In *Teacher*, the dialogue and many of the gags relate directly to the staffroom issues of the day. *Nurse*, his favourite Carry On, reflects everyone's hospital experiences. Many of its comic incidents were provided by his wife Rita, who spent seven years as a nurse. Hudis recalls that if he was stuck, he had only to shout downstairs and ask Rita what other funny things she remembered. Hudis excels in what Thomas describes as 'heart'. In *Nurse*, for example, Kenneth Williams' reaction to Matron's inexplicable demand that he should not lie on top of the bedclothes is the kind of crushing riposte with which every ex-patient can identify. 'If a doctor asks me to hang by one arm from the ceiling wearing an aqualung, with my birthday tattooed on my left buttock in shorthand, I'll do it. He aims to cure me. Your rule has nothing to do with my cure, therefore it has no meaning in here'. He throws himself lengthwise on top of the bedclothes and adds, in his most supercilious voice, 'Now, I wish to rest.'

The script of *Nurse*, like those of *Sergeant*, *Constable* and *Cruising*, originally ended in typical Hudis togetherness, with Terence Longden and Shirley Eaton romantically paired and everyone's problems solved. It was Thomas who decided during editing to pull the famous daffodil joke out of the middle and use it as a climax. In doing so he created a classic ending which went beyond Hudis, and later films always ended with a dash of sauce.

Just as Hudis was preparing to leave for Hollywood, Talbot Rothwell offered Rogers a script called *Follow That Cab*. It was not intended as a Carry On but its storyline and casting were so similar that it was released as *Carry On Cabby* and has become one of the key films of the series.

Rothwell was already an established scriptwriter when he joined the Carry On team. He had written for the Crazy Gang and had scripted radio and TV shows for Terry-Thomas, Arthur Askey and Ted Ray. His stage comedies, *Queen Elizabeth Slept Here, Once Upon a Crime* and *Meet the Wife*, had successful West End runs.

According to a profile he once wrote about himself, Rothwell 'was born at an early age to mixed parentage – one father and one mother' in 1916, in Bromley, Kent. He claimed to have invented his first ghastly pun at the age of nine when, after a disastrous newt-fishing trip, he commented 'No newts is good newts'. His early career in the Thirties, as successively, a clerk at Brighton Town Hall, a member of the Palestine Police force and an RAF pilot, gave little indication of any show biz potential. It was during the war, when he was forced to bale out over German-occupied Norway and spent several years in a prisoner-of-war camp, that he was bitten by the entertainment bug. He wrote, performed and MC-ed for the camp theatre, and at one time organized a raucous show to mask the noises made by escapers. Fellow prison-camp entertainers included Rupert Davies, later famous as TV's Maigret, and Carry On's Peter Butterworth.

Talbot Rothwell

'Tolly' to his friends, he wrote scripts for 20 of the 29 Carry On films. His first script, *Cabby*, is very much in the Hudis mould, but although the basic formula never changed, his style became both bluer and wilder. Rothwell wasn't a writer of carefully sewn-up plotlines. His narratives were as unbridled and anarchic as his sense of humour. He had seen many of the great music hall comics, and was a great admirer of Max Miller, whose risqué routines were legendary. Rothwell saw the series as an extension of the real music hall which a younger generation had never seen. He concentrated much of his energy on those corny double entendres and mind-boggling puns. In the Hudis scripts the blue jokes were no more than a decoration, but in Rothwell's hands they became the very fabric of the film.

Gerald Thomas, Phil Silvers and Peter Rogers celebrate the first day of shooting on *Follow That Camel*.

The famous dinner scene from *Up The Khyber* is a classic of the series – a delightfully wicked spoof on the concept of the British stiff upper lip, as the band plays on.

Here are two typical examples. In *Matron*, Hattie Jacques (in the title role) tells Dr Cutting (Kenneth Williams), 'I'm a simple woman with simple tastes. I want to be wooed'. To which Williams replies, 'You can be as wude as you like with me'. In *Henry*, Marie of Normandy (Joan Sims) is distraught when Sir Roger de Lodgerley (Charles Hawtrey) is threatened with the thumbscrew. 'Fear not, madam', declares the bold Sir Roger, 'I can stand any amount of screwing.'

Rothwell's deftness with saucily daft names – the Khazi of Kalibar, Citizen Bidet, Senna Pod, Emmannuelle Prevert, Jock Strapp – adds to the fun. 'By this time tomorrow', says Citizen Camembert, standing gleefully by the guillotine in *Don't Lose Your Head*, 'the Duke of Pomfritte will have had his chips'. After the mock French puns, there were mock Latin ones in *Cleo*, with Marcus and Spencius taking pride of place. And who but Rothwell would think of naming an avenue Avery for no other reason than the pleasure of giving *Screaming's* Sergeant Bung the immortal line, 'Then we must explore Avery Avenue'?

It was Rothwell, too, who was responsible for the introduction of the outrageous secondary titles, like *Mind My Chopper* (Henry) or *Womb At The Top* (Matron). His jokes, he used to say, were bawdy but never really dirty. 'I have what you might call self-imposed rules. Nobody ever actually swears. And nobody ever actually succeeds in getting into bed with anyone else.'

After Rothwell's untimely death, the next three films, *Behind*, *England* and *Emmannuelle*, caught up with the permissive society, and became a great deal more explicit.

The Music

Music has always played an important role in the Carry Ons, adding another strand to the visual and verbal humour. The musical jokes range from the corny to the classical. In *Cabby* the orchestra plays 'Oh dear, what can the matter be' when a front door is opened to reveal a lone toilet. In *Up The Khyber* Tchaikovsky's 'Letter Song' can be heard when Sir Sidney Ruff-Diamond is dictating a letter to Queen Victoria.

Bruce Montgomery

The first Carry On music maestro was Bruce Montgomery, a scholarly Cambridge type who wrote detective stories under the pseudonym Edmund Crispin and whose tippling habits were legendary. He was at his best with the lively march music for *Sergeant*, played by the band of the Coldstream Guards; and the wonderfully aggressive theme which accompanies Hattie Jacques' Matron as she sweeps along the corridors in *Nurse*.

Eric Rogers

Montgomery was less at home with creative ideas, and would often call on the help of a jobbing musician, Eric Rogers. As a result Montgomery was frequently late with his scores, and eventually Peter Rogers decided to bring Eric Rogers into the team. It was the beginning of a long and fruitful relationship between the two men who, incidentally, are not related.

Eric's musical education began at the age of 13 when he was taught by the local organist. During his wartime service with the RAF he played the piano, which earned him free beer – a useful musical apprenticeship. With his demobilization gratuity, he formed a small orchestra which played in the Orchid Room at the London Trocadero. After working as an arranger-accompanist for, among others, Fred Emney and Julie Wilson, he began composing background music for films. He started with children's films and then moved to features, including *The Wooden Horse* (1950), *Encore* (1951) and *Genevieve* (1953). He wrote the theme song for TV's *Sunday Night at the London Palladium* and was the musical director of several variety theatres. When Lionel Bart thought up the music for *Oliver*, he sent for Rogers to write it down and make the arrangements. He worked on several stage musicals, arranged a number of hits in the United States (among them 'Apple Blossom Time' by Rosemary June) and released some popular long-playing records.

Peter Rogers, on the other hand, has no musical education but is devoted to music. It's a passion which goes back to his childhood, when he used to turn the pages while his father played the piano. He taught himself to read music at the age of 21 and has since developed a wide taste and knowledge in the field. He plays the piano, organ and balalaika and is something of a composer himself, having contributed to the theme music for the Joan Collins film, *Quest for Love* (1970).

Eric composed and conducted the music for 22 Carry On films, often consulting Peter, who was always ready with ideas. The resulting scores have their own humour which supports the main action and never works against it. Sometimes the score indulges in the kind of satire which everyone can appreciate, like the playing of 'Greensleeves' in *Henry*, or the warning note sounded by 'Do Not Trust Him, Gentle Maiden' when Lady Ponsonby (Angela Douglas) is willingly abducted by Abdul Abulbul (Bernard Bresslaw) in *Follow That Camel*. Some jokes are culled from popular TV programmes; the theme music from both *Z Cars* and *Steptoe and Son* is echoed in *Screaming*. Others are more obscure, like the choice of 'The Unhatched Chicks' from Moussorgsky's 'Pictures From an Exhibition' in *Doctor* when Mrs Barron (Gwendolyn Watts) comes to collect her husband (Charles Hawtrey) who has been suffering from a sympathetic pregnancy. And there is at least one 'in' joke – a Scott Joplin-style rag, composed around the initial letters of Peter's wife, BEB (Betty Evelyn Box) which can be heard in *Girls*.

Eric also wrote the songs which introduce *Cowboy*, *Screaming* and *Don't Lose Your Head*. He was a gifted and versatile instrumentalist who became great friends with his producer. He was writing a book about music when he died in 1977. 'I was rather lost', says Peter, 'when he died; I had no-one to talk to about music.'

Sidney James

'The general appearance of an ancient and dissipated walnut', said Hattie Jacques about Sidney James' face in *Carry On Loving*. Various critics have likened his face to 'an overworked punchbag', 'an army assault course' and 'something heaped, hewn and furrowed by a medieval craftsman'. Sid himself compared it to 'a bed that has been slept in with the sheets left rumpled'.

Freddie Mills, calling in at the Helping Hands Agency in *Carry On Regardless*, puts it more simply: 'I'd know that ugly mug anywhere'. 'You've got to admit', Sid once confessed, 'this ugly mug of mine has gone a long way towards getting me where I am today'.

It's not only the face, of course, but also that gravel-crunching Cockney voice, the filthy, lecherous yuk-yuk of a laugh and the beer-and-betting shop mannerisms which shaped his unique stage, radio and screen personality and kept him at the centre of the action through 19 Carry Ons.

The special joy of Sid's Carry On performances is that whatever the role – be it a king in *Henry*, a colonial governor in *Up The Khyber*, a white hunter in *Up The Jungle*, a petty thief in *Matron* or a taxi-owner in *Cabby* – he remains the familiar chuckling, womanizing, streetwise Sid. Or to put it another way, as Frankie Howerd says in *Up The Jungle*, 'he's as common as muck'.

'They bung a beard on me', Sid said on the set of *Henry*, 'give me plumes and things and dress me up in ruddy heavy costumes – but I'm still me.'

In *Dick*, where he has two roles to play, he seems less at home as the quiet-spoken Reverend Flasher than as the daring highwayman Big Dick. In *Don't Lose Your Head*, his original identity as the lisping Sir Rodney Ffing – 'that doodling, dandy-prat' as Citizen Camembert calls him – sits less easily than his guises and disguises as the dashing Black Fingernail.

'Get me a nice double room with hot and cold running chambermaids', he tells the hotel clerk in *Girls* – a request which neatly sums up the lip-smacking lechery of Sid's personality. As often as not, it's his roving eye which gets him into trouble. In *Henry*, the arrival of Barbara Windsor as the saucy Bettina puts all thoughts of his Queen (Joan Sims) out of his mind. In *Loving*, it is the flighty Joan Sims who tempts him to stray from the homelier pleasures offered by Hattie Jacques. His screen flirtations with Barbara Windsor provide some of his cheekiest Carry On moments, although after *Camping* the censor became increasingly concerned that Sid was getting too old to chat up young girls on film for family audiences. The most endearing moments stem from his on/off relationship with Hattie Jacques, most notably in *Cabby*, when it is work, not women, which keeps them apart.

His one and only role as a 'baddie', the Rumpo Kid in *Cowboy*, is a little different from the rest. A kind of comic realism takes over, and Sid sports an American accent and a cowboy swagger. This was his favourite Carry On. 'It gave me a chance to do some horse riding, which I love', he said at the time, 'as well as all sorts of things that were different for me . . . It was like going back to the type of parts I used to play before I started this light comedy stuff'.

Above: in *Again Doctor*, Sid is at his seediest as Gladstone Screwer, resident of the benighted Beatific Islands, who discovers a remarkably effective slimming aid which, when marketed in England, makes money – and trouble – for all concerned.

Above right: in his first ever Carry On venture, Sid played Sergeant Wilkins, the long-suffering copper who had to deal with three incompetent recruits let loose on his beat in *Constable*. Luckily, he has the shoulder of Sergeant Moon (Hattie Jacques) to cry on.

Right: 'Bless you, my son', says Sid Boggle (Sid James) in *Camping*. No, Carry On's favourite rake has not changed the habits of a lifetime – he is still chasing the girls, even in this unlikely disguise.

Critics who have described him as a natural have got it wrong. They have underestimated the degree of professionalism, experience and acumen which goes into the making of 'this light comedy stuff'. Sid worked hard on stage and screen before he hit the big time in *Hancock's Half Hour* and in the Carry Ons.

Born in Johannesburg in 1913, he was introduced to showbusiness as a small boy, performing with his parents, a music-hall team. He didn't take acting seriously, however, until much later. As a young man he had a variety of jobs – hairdresser, roller-skater, dance instructor, stevedore, coal heaver and diamond polisher. In later life, he used to regale his friends with colourful stories of his days as a middleweight boxer, and would point to his thrice-broken nose and cauliflower ears as evidence.

During the war, he served as a lieutenant in an anti-tank regiment in the Middle East, but was also in an entertainment unit, which fired his determination to go into showbusiness. He spent his service gratuity on travelling to England to try his luck.

After the usual round of repertory, his Cockney voice and breezy personality earned him his first screen role as an East End bandleader in the crime melodrama *It Always Rains on Sunday* (1947). A number of character parts followed in films like *The Lavender Hill Mob* (1951), *A Kid for Two Farthings* (1955) and Carol Reed's *Trapeze* (1956). At the same time, he was making his way in stage musicals, as a gangster in *Kiss Me Kate* and in the lead in a West End production of *Guys and Dolls*.

He achieved nationwide fame in the radio programme *Hancock's Half Hour*, which started in 1956. His gravelly voice and down-to-earth personality made him the perfect foil for Tony Hancock's outer-suburban flights of fancy. After five years on radio and another three on TV, the partnership finally broke up. 'I don't think Tony will be as funny without me', he said at the time, 'I know I won't be as funny without him'. Nevertheless, Sid was successful with his own TV series, including *Citizen James*, *Taxi* and the still-repeated *Bless This House*.

'The two best things that happened in my working life', he often used to say, 'were Tony Hancock and the Carry Ons'. Starting with *Constable*, he played in 19, as well as countless other films, the exact number of which depends on who's counting – 180 according to *The Times*' obituary, 250 according to *The Daily Mail* and 280 from the pen of an enthusiastic blurb-writer for *Dick*.

Popular and sociable, his hardworking, hard-drinking, hard-betting lifestyle took its toll. In the mid-Sixties he suffered a massive heart attack and was forced to ease up. He was in such poor health during the making of *Doctor* that he played all his scenes in bed. But, Gerald Thomas comments, 'that was Sid, and he carried on living in the way that he wanted.'

He continued to enjoy a busy social and professional life, and in the early Seventies made a brilliantly successful tour with *The Mating Season* in Australia, where it broke all box-office records and he was voted Best Actor by the critics. Its British production, at the Sunderland Empire in 1976, was Sid's last. He collapsed on stage in front of the first-night audience and died on his way to hospital.

Among the warm and emotional tributes which poured in, Barbara Windsor's summed up the feelings of many of the Carry On team: 'He was wonderful to work with', she said. 'He *was* the Carry On films'.

Top: Sid Fiddler (Sid) is caught in a compromising position with Miss Easy Rider, otherwise known as Hope Springs (Barbara Windsor), in *Girls*. But what else can you expect when the enterprising Sid organises a beauty competition.

Right: in *Cowboy*, Sid played his only real baddie of the series, The Rumpo Kid, the scourge of Stodge City, seen here facing the final showdown at high noon.

Tributes to Sid James Died 26th April, 1976

'I just can't believe it. Out of all the people I know in show business Sid was such a gentleman. He was just wonderful and I loved him so much.'

Barbara Windsor

'Sid was known in the business as 'one-take James' because what ever he did he always did first time – and did it right. In the Hancock's Half Hour days he was a tremendous support to Tony Hancock; a really great professional.'

Ray Galton (Galton and Simpson)

'The only thing that ever frightened him was, believe it or not, radio. I remember the first time we did Hancock on radio, Sid was so scared that he wore a trilby hat pulled down over his head and had the scripts arranged on a stand so that he could hide behind them. One day a gust of wind blew the scripts over the whole studio. There was just something he hated about doing radio in front of an audience. We never found out what it was.'

Alan Simpson (Galton and Simpson)

'Sid James was a rare bird. He wasn't much of a comedian and he wasn't much of an actor – he was something much more. He always spoke directly to the audience and whatever he did gave a kind of deep feeling to the people watching him.'

Frank Muir

'He belied his brash image and all the things he looked like. In fact he was a very kind man – yes, and chivalrous. That old fashioned word really applied to him. He cared for all his friends and they cared very much for him.'

Hattie Jacques

'He was a super person to get on with, he had great comedy timing, and he was a very generous actor. He always encouraged young people. He never upstaged anyone. We've lost a fine comedy talent, and I have lost a great friend.'

Gerald Thomas

'Sid James was the Anchor Man of the Carry On films. He didn't mind what he played, large parts or small parts, so long as he was in them. That's how he felt and that's how we felt. There was always that sense of safety with Sid around. He was such a unique personality that when he died a certain element of the Carry On formula died with him, an element that has always been very difficult to replace. So difficult, in fact, that the best policy seemed to be not to try to replace him. That in itself, surely, is sufficient tribute to the quality and value of Sid James as an artiste.'

Peter Rogers

Captain Wellington (Sid James) in *Cruising* is mixing his drinks in search of the formula dreamed up by a favourite barman.

Carry On Years: 1960–1974 **Carry On Films:** 19

Carry On Titles: Constable; Regardless; Cruising; Cabby; Cleo; Cowboy; Don't Lose Your Head; Doctor; Up The Khyber; Again Doctor; Camping; Up The Jungle; Loving; Henry; At Your Convenience; Abroad; Matron; Girls; Dick.

Carry On Professions: police sergeant; employment agency manager; ship's captain; cab owner; Roman nobleman; outlaw; aristocrat; governor of Indian province; medical officer; big game hunter; proprietor, marriage bureau; monarch; factory foreman; publican; petty thief; beauty contest organizer; highwayman; clergyman.

A running Carry On gag, repeated in many entries in the series, is the never-to-be-resolved relationship between Hattie and Kenneth Williams, seen her in a scene from *Matron*.

Hattie Jacques

Hattie Jacques was a grand person in more than one sense of the word – grand in figure, grand-hearted and a grand professional on stage, radio and screen.

In life, as her fellow-artistes testify, she was an extraordinarily kind and gentle person. On screen her image was often more formidable. For most Carry On fans, the indelible memory of her is as Matron in *Carry On Nurse*, storming along the corridors with that Victorian 'we are not amused' glint in her eye, striking terror in the hearts of everyone in her path.

The warning cry, 'Matron's round!' is enough to send patients and nurses scurrying to their proper places – although it also leads to such cracks as 'Mine's a pint' from Bill Owen, or 'I don't care if she's triangular' from Terence Longden.

Although she was five times a Carry On Matron (in *Nurse*, *Camping*, *Doctor*, *Again Doctor* and *Matron*), a Sister in *Regardless* and a martinet of a schoolmarm in *Teacher*, she was by no means stuck with the battle-axe image. In the Carry On world, buxom may sometimes be beautiful but outsize is usually outrageous – which gave her scope for some splendid portrayals of unrequited passion. In *Doctor* and *Matron* she handled this stereotype with comic sensitivity which was never embarrassing because it was always tinged with pathos. But she had a way with one-liners, too. 'I was once a weak man', says Kenneth Williams, as she makes a grab for him in *Doctor*. 'Once a week is enough for any man', she replies sternly.

Part of her charm flows from the contrast between her imposing figure and her plaintive, little-girl voice. Her ability to combine broad comedy with pathos was particularly endearing in her role as the neglected wife of a workaholic taxi-owner in *Cabby*. To capture his attention, she sets up a rival taxi firm and drives him off the streets. Her recognition that she has won the war but may have lost a husband is a truly touching moment.

Her role in *At Your Convenience* is largely irrelevant to the main narrative, but it is the high point of the comedy. She plays a housewife devoted to her budgerigar and obsessed with the desire to make it talk. 'A mesmerically funny colloquy with a budgerigar' is how the *New Statesman* film critic described the scene.

In *Abroad* she displayed another side of her screen personality as the fiery, kitchen-bound wife of the demented hotel manager (Peter Butterworth) – a Latin whirlwind, angrily stoking the stove and stirring the pots, dressed in dirndl skirt and peasant blouse, with a mass of black Spanish kiss-curls.

Hattie Jacques was born in Sandgate, Kent, in 1924. She trained as a hairdresser but during the war worked first as a nurse and then as an arc welder at a North London factory. It was here that she discovered her talent for making people laugh – to some extent a defensive talent, since from earliest days she had to learn to cope with being larger than life.

Right: in *At Your Convenience*, Hattie gives a warm and well-observed performance as the housebound wife whose only company is her budgie.

Below: in *Again Doctor*, Gladstone Screwer (Sid James) makes improper advances towards the stern and upright Matron (Hattie, of course).

When her brother took a job as a lift-operator at London's celebrated Little Players' Theatre, she went along too. Soon she was on stage, singing Victorian songs at the Players' popular late-night reviews and giving high-spirited performances in their pantomimes and plays. It was at the Players that she developed her famous Christmas Fairy persona, and for many years she appeared annually as an outsize fairy: Fairy Antedota, Fairy Fragrant in her own version of a Victorian Cinderella, and the Fairy Queen in 'The Sleeping Beauty in the Wood', which she often used to mention as her favourite role. Throughout her career she remained faithful to the Players' Theatre, returning to it whenever she could as performer, producer and occasionally as writer. She also toured with the Old Vic.

Like several of the Carry On team, she first gained fame on radio. Her little-girl voice came into its own for Sophie Tuckshop, the greedy schoolgirl addicted to mammoth

Above: Kenneth Williams and Hattie are at it again, this time in *Camping* when the headmaster is lured unsuspectingly into the wrong washrooms to the consternation of the outraged Miss Haggerd.

Above right: Hattie contributes a wonderful cameo to *Abroad* as Floella, the harassed cook of the Elsbels Hotel, bossed by the even more harassed Pepe (Peter Butterworth).

Right: the formidable Miss Haggerd (Hattie Jacques) leads the school party (including the bouncy Babs, played by Barbara Windsor) to their morning ablutions in *Camping*.

meals, in Tommy Handley's *ITMA* (It's That Man Again), a series which kept people at home by the radio in the Forties. She then had a spell as Agatha Danglebody in *Educating Archie* where she met Eric Sykes who had contributed some of the scripts. This was the beginning of a 30-year partnership with Sykes, as his long-suffering sister, in a succession of TV series which were so popular, and so much part of people's lives, that many believed they really were brother and sister. She was also involved in some of the *Hancock's Half Hours*. She latterly devoted herself almost exclusively to radio, TV and films. Among her more serious film roles were appearances in *Nicholas Nickleby* (1947), *Oliver Twist* (1948) and as Nanette Parry in *Make Mine Mink* (1960).

Because of her imposing figure, Hattie was usually typecast, and many of her friends believed that her talents were never fully exploited. She remained philosophical

about her size. She sometimes expressed a yearning to look more 'normal', once shedding four stone. But when she arrived at the TV studio nobody noticed the difference, so she abandoned all thoughts of dieting. 'When you're my size', she once said, 'you're conditioned from childhood to people making jokes against you. You have to learn to make them laugh with you, rather than at you,' and in this she was a supreme artist.

She was loved by everybody who worked with her. When she died, Eric Sykes said that she had been like a real sister to him. And she was a continual source of comfort and affection on the Carry On sets. Everyone seemed to run to her with their troubles. 'She never lost her temper', said Barbara Windsor, 'and was always helping people with their problems'. Joan Sims was particularly close to her and Hattie gave her a lot of moral and practical support during a particularly stressful period in her life.

She was a generous hostess and thought nothing of inviting everyone home, after a long hard day on the set, and cooking them a meal. At Christmas and New Year, single members of the Carry On team, like Kenneth Williams and Joan Sims, always had somewhere to go, and she presided over wonderful Christmas and New Year parties.

'If she had one fault', her agent Felix de Wolfe said, 'it was that she could easily be put upon. She was getting constant requests to do charity work, like personal appearances and opening bazaars, and she'd try to attend every one'.

Hattie Jacques was married to actor John le Mesurier. They had two sons and although they later divorced, they remained on good terms with each other. Her sudden death in October 1980 was a tremendous loss for British comedy and left a gap in the Carry Ons which can never be filled.

Carry On Years: 1959–1974 **Carry On Films:** 14

Carry On Titles: Sergeant; Nurse; Teacher; Constable; Regardless; Cabby; Doctor; Again Doctor; Camping; Loving; At Your Convenience; Abroad; Matron; Dick.

Carry On Professions: army medical officer; hospital matron; teacher; policewoman; hospital sister; cab owner; school matron; marriage bureau proprietor; housewife; cook; housekeeper; church organist.

Tributes to Hattie Jacques
Died 6th October, 1980

'She was one of the very best – and was like a real sister to me. I first met Hattie on the radio show "Educating Archie" in 1950. I knew from that one performance that she was a natural. Her great strength was that she could make any script come alive immediately. Her voice, her professionalism, her manner, and her humour were original. She was one of the very best comedy actresses we have ever had and a very lovely lady.

Eric Sykes

'I can hardly pick the words to express my shock and grief. We have always remained affectionate friends. She was a kindly, wonderful woman who would help anybody.'

John Le Mesurier (her former husband)

'I was always trying to get her to take life a bit easier. If she had a fault it was that she could easily be put upon. She was getting constant requests to do charity work, like personal appearances and opening bazaars, and she'd try to attend every one. She was gracious, considerate and her kindness was renowned. She became a big star, yet remained a very modest woman and totally unchanged from the day I first met her.'

Felix de Wolfe (her agent)

'She was the sort of person one warmed to immediately. She was blessed with a marvellous personality, tremendous charm and a consideration for all those on the film set. We had unforgettable times together.'

Kenneth Williams

'Hattie Jacques was a large lady in more ways than one. Not only was she a large lady in size she was a large lady in heart. She was what you might call the Mother Superior of the Carry On family. She would sit doing *The Times* crossword (successfully, I might say) and first one and then another of the cast would sit beside her and unburden himself or herself to her. Hattie would listen carefully and then quietly dispense her advice. That is the sort of person she was – a tower of strength, kind, generous, understanding, with a wonderful sense of humour.'

Peter Rogers

Kenneth Williams

'Infamy... Infamy... they've all got it in for me...'

Above: the Khasi of Kalabar (Kenneth) holds up for all to see the undisputed and incriminating evidence of cowardice in the Third Foot and Mouth Regiment in *Up The Khyber*.

Above left: Caesar's enemies have finally done for him in *Cleo*. This was one of Kenneth Williams' most delightfully outrageous roles.

Constables Benson and Gorse (Kenneth Williams and Charles Hawtrey) are dressed to kill as they stalk a shoplifter in *Constable*.

Kenneth Williams' death in April 1988 robbed the series of its longest-running 'regular'. In the Carry On roll-call he is the champion. He had 25 films to his credit (plus the commentary, shared with Barbara Windsor, of *That's Carry On*) beating Joan Sims, at 24, by a short head. Step by step through the series, from *Sergeant* to *Emmannuelle*, he developed a comic personality which started as a good-looking, self-confident young egg-head with a supercilious air and became a nostril-flaring, eye-popping, pompous and conceited ass.

In the early Carry Ons he possesses an eccentric charm as a know-all who never suffers fools gladly but who is

Above: in *Matron*, Kenneth plays Sir Bernard Cutter, the hypochondriacal surgeon who has only to read about a disease to think that he's got it.

always around to take the initiative when leadership is required. He is usually eager to please – so eager that he fails to realize the mess he's making of his relationship with his superiors. In *Sergeant*, he is the snobbish recruit who distances himself from the barrack-room frolics but eventually uses his knowledge of sociology to pull the unit together. In *Nurse*, he is a physics student and the only patient to have the nerve – and the self-righteousness – to stand up to Matron. Later, he masterminds the patients' do-it-yourself operation. (It is also the only Carry On in which he indulges in a genuine bit of light romance.) In *Constable*, he's a beady-eyed rookie who fancies his ability to judge criminal faces – a self-deception which results in aid to a jewel thief and the arrest of a CID man.

In *Regardless*, he is the intellectual of the Helping Hands agency, displaying a delightful arrogance when taking a pet ape for a walk across London. This is Williams at his most charming.

Spying, in which he uses his well-known comic radio voice, marks the change from campus superciliousness to suburban camp. In the historicals he camps it up further with increasingly manic portrayals as he moves from Julius Caesar in *Cleo* (introduced with the line 'Oh I do feel queer') to the mincing, hypocritical Citizen Camembert in *Don't Lose Your Head* and the power-mad Khazi of Kalibar in *Up The Khyber*.

There is an inherent madness about his doctor roles, whether it's the surgeon Carver in *Again Doctor*, terrified that others will steal a march on him, or the frantic hypochondriacal Sir Bernard Cutter in *Matron* who has only to hear about an illness to imagine he is dying from it. Always a reluctant screen lover, he provokes great fun and games when, in *Doctor*, *Matron* and *Camping*, he has to flee from the unwanted attentions of Hattie Jacques. This relationship was so much a part of the hospital Carry Ons that in *Camping* Matron makes a cheeky reference back to one of her previous infatuations with Williams.

As the series developed, Williams became the master of the double entendre, sometimes delivered slyly and knowingly, often more innocently but always tongue in cheek.

In the later Carry On films, when a more permissive audience was targeted, some of the films take a direct

Left: 'There's a whole in my desert!' wails Commandant Burger (Kenneth Williams) when he and his men finally arrive at a waterhole after a long and thirsty trek.
Above: one of Kenneth Williams warmest cameos occurs in *Regardless* when he is assigned to look after a chimp.
Below: a timely sneeze denudes Citizen Camembert (Kenneth Williams) of his wig in *Don't Lose Your Head.*

In his autobiography **Just Williams**, Kenneth Williams recalls that during the shooting of the scene in **Carry On Constable** in which Joan Sims inadvertently enters the men's dressing-room and they all retreat naked, the studio lights made their bottoms look as if they were alight. Gerald Thomas summoned the make-up department for a powdering session, which provoked some irritation and a lot of ribaldry. 'I've done Margaret Lockwood and I've done Jean Kent and I've done some of the best faces in the business,' said one of the make-up men, 'but I never thought I'd end up doing a bum'.

camp delight in exposing his rear view, notably in *Behind* and *Emmannuelle* – 'a treat' as the *Films and Filming* critic put it 'for which I'm not sure the cinema audiences are altogether ready'.

Like several other Carry On-ers, Williams' first claim to fame was as a radio entertainer. Born in 1926, he trained as a lithographer, acting in his spare time with the amateur Tavistock Repertory Theatre. During the Second World War he served in India, then toured Malaya and Burma as part of the Combined Entertainments Unit. It was his contact with entertainers in the army, especially Stanley Baxter (who became a life-long friend), which prompted him to try his hand in the world of show business.

He worked in repertory for several years until his performance in *Henry VI* in Birmingham attracted attention. He signed on with the Old Vic but after a week's rehearsal was released from his contract at his own request, having chosen instead to appear in the TV version of H.G. Wells' *Wonderful Visit*. He appeared regularly on the stage and in cabaret, but it was in radio shows like Kenneth Horne's *Round the Horn* and *Beyond Our Ken*, and later *Hancock's Half-Hour* (with Sid James and Hattie Jacques) that his inimitable voice became immediately recognizable to millions of households, particularly when uttering his

Tributes to Kenneth Williams · Died 25th April 1988

'When I heard of the death of Kenneth Williams I thought that this is too much. It shouldn't have happened. I couldn't believe it. He was so full of life, such wonderful company, how could he ever die?

'It's odd, isn't it, how we always want nice things to last forever? Not so odd, really, I suppose. It's like the trick we used to indulge in when we were kids – leaving the best bits on the plate until the end. That's how I felt about Kenneth Williams. He was the life and soul of any function he attended and for me it was always a happy day when he was "on call" at the Studio.'

Peter Rogers

'Kenneth was a gentleman in all respects. He was a very generous performer and gave 100 per cent, whether on or off screen. He had no time for unprofessional conduct on the set and was held with great affection by his fellow artists. He was a wonderful storyteller and kept us in fits of laughter off stage, particularly when reminiscing with Kenneth Connor and Joan Sims.

'As part of the "Carry On" team Kenneth is irreplaceable, and as a great and much loved friend of mine, is sadly missed.'

Gerald Thomas

'If he came out head down and hunched up you knew you were in for trouble. You'd go to a restaurant and he'd start complaining. He'd complain loudly that the food was dreadful – then after you'd been through hell, he'd sit back with his little-boy look and say, "Mmmm, quite nice here, isn't it?".'

Barbara Windsor

famous catchphrase 'stop messing about'.

Kenneth was deeply upset when Hancock, in his never-ending attempt to strip his act down to the basic essentials, dropped him from the cast. His subsequent work as compère and stand-up comic for *International Cabaret*, with his long, circuitous, anarchistic introductions, earned him a cult following which resulted in his own programmes *The Kenneth Williams Show* and *Stop Messing About*. He particularly enjoyed children's entertainment and was a regular on *Jackanory*; he was a frequent guest on TV chat shows and a witty and erudite contributor to radio's panel game *Just a Minute*.

His film career began after Peter Rogers spotted him in the successful stage show *Share My Lettuce* and signed him up for *Sergeant*. He played in numerous films, including two others for Rogers – *Raising the Wind* (1961) and *Twice Round the Daffodils* (1962), both of which were directed by Gerald Thomas.

He was a close friend of the controversial playwright, Joe Orton, playing Inspector Trusscott in the original Cambridge production of his *Loot*. He was devastated by Orton's violent death.

Kenneth would only accept parts with which he felt comfortable. Over the years, he came to prefer TV and films to stage work. He didn't like the unsocial hours of the theatre and no longer relished doing the same thing, night after night, with the same people. 'You're a prisoner for six nights a week and one matinée', he said. 'It's different with the Carry Ons. Every time the team get together it's like a family reunion'.

Kenneth's tastes and talents were many-sided. He wrote several books, including an autobiographical series which includes *Just Williams*, *Acid Drops*, *Back Drops* and *I Only Have to Close My Eyes*. He had a sensitivity for music, poetry and painting and was deeply religious.

On the set, he would often ease the tension by regaling the cast and crew with a stream of anecdotes and impersonations. But he remained undoubtedly the most idiosyncratic member of the team.

His books reveal him as a complex and self-absorbed personality, yet he clearly fitted into a team whose members are chosen not only for their comedy talents but also for their ability to get on with one another, without anyone pulling rank.

Carry On Years: 1958–1978 **Carry On Films:** 25

Carry On Titles: Sergeant; Nurse; Teacher; Constable; Regardless; Cruising, Jack; Spying; Cleo; Cowboy; Screaming; Don't Lose Your Head; Follow That Camel; Doctor; Up The Khyber; Again Doctor; Camping; Loving; Henry; At Your Convenience; Abroad; Matron; Dick; Behind; Emmannuelle.

Carry On Professions: soldier; physics boffin; teacher; policeman; helping hand; ship's officer; ship's captain; secret agent; emperor; judge; scientist; chief of secret police; Foreign Legion officer; doctor; rajah; surgeon; marriage counsellor; courtier; factory owner; courier; Bow Street runner; archaeologist; ambassador.

Charles Hawtrey

Charles Hawtrey first trod the boards in 1925, a debut which makes him the Carry On-er with the longest showbusiness record. By the time he was signed up for *Carry On Sergeant*, he had already made a name for himself in films, revues, pantomime and on the stage and had produced several shows of his own. Many of the elements which go into his Carry On personality can be traced back to his earlier years.

He was born in November 1914, the son of the light-comedy actor-manager, Sir Charles Hawtrey, who was celebrated for his immaculate man-about-town roles and won his knighthood for his services to theatre. Charles Hawtrey is immensely proud of his father and when he is in

Right: Charles Hawtrey makes a fetching Lady Puddleton in *Again Doctor*. He is really Dr Stoppage, trying to infiltrate a nursing home in the only way he knows how.

Below: Cromwell (Kenneth Williams) inflicts a wholly painful torture on Sir Roger de Lodgerley (Charles Hawtrey) in *Henry*.

Right: Special Constable Gorse (Charles Hawtrey) is something of a trial to his superiors in *Sergeant*. 'I haven't done this since the army when I was in a camp concert', he says on parade.

Charles Hawtrey: These films haven't made me rich but they've given me a world-wide identity.

the mood delights in telling anecdotes about him. Well into middle age he was still billed as Charles Hawtrey Jnr, in deference to his father's memory.

With such a family background it was natural for the young Charles to be given an early stage training. He spent three years at the prestigious Italia Conti acting school and was soon launched into the profession in a variety of junior roles. His 1925 debut was as a street urchin in *The Windmill Man*, at Boscombe. His first London roles were the White Cat and the Bootblack in *Bluebell in Fairyland*, and he appeared in *Where the Rainbow Ends* and *Peter Pan*. He is proud of the fact that his film record goes back to 1930, when he appeared in the silent film *Marry Me*. Throughout the 1930s and 1940s he appeared in dozens of revues, pantomimes, comedies and classical plays, including the Old Vic production of *The Taming of the Shrew*. But the durability of film, and frequent TV repeats, have ensured that he is best remembered at this stage of his career as the elderly schoolboy in the Will Hay screen classics *Good Morning Boys* (1937) and *The Goose Steps Out* (1942). The eternal schoolboy image which he created in those earlier days helped to shape his screen personality in TV's *The Army Game* and in the Carry Ons.

His Carry On personality emerged fully formed in his first

role, as Private Golightly in *Sergeant*. He is a bespectacled, weedy eager-beaver who skips happily through life with a child-like unawareness of the dotty impression he is creating on others. As a patient in *Nurse* he spends most of his time locked into earphones, playing at being a conductor when he listens to classical music, giggling loudly at a comedy or weeping into his pillow throughout a play, always totally oblivious of the chaos around him. As a trainee policeman in *Constable*, and a learner taxi-driver (aptly known as 'Pint-Pot') in *Cabby*, he has that same boyish enthusiasm for the job on hand, desperate to please and completely unfazed when things inevitably go wrong. In *Camping* he inadvertently pitches his tent on an army firing range, where it is swiftly blown away. 'I knew I shouldn't have eaten those radishes', is his explanation.

This aspect of his screen personality reached a peak in *Up The Khyber*. As the kilted Private Widdle of the Third Foot and Mouth Brigade, on sentry-duty at the farm-gate which stands in good stead for the Khyber Pass, he cheerfully chatters away to Bungdit Dinn (Bernard Bres-slaw), the hostile Indian Burpa, and allows himself to be bonked on the head and stripped of his incriminating woolly underpants.

With his drainpipe figure and a fluting camped-up voice, Hawtrey can hardly be classed as a sex symbol. When it seems as if he is about to embark on a clandestine love affair, he is really involved in the flip side of one of Talbot Rothwell's cheeky double entendres and is, in fact, about to share his evening with a woman over a game of cards or a spot of telly-viewing. But as well as typecasting him, the Carry On productions have taken a satirical delight in putting him into the most unlikely roles – as the lecherous Sir Roger de Lodgerly, the queen's lover and the father of her heir in *Henry*; the pedantic, peaceloving Indian chief Big Heap in *Cowboy*; or The Great Tonka, Father of Countless, in the all-woman realm of Aphrodisia in *Up The Jungle*.

An ideal candidate for drag, his female impersonation is particularly effective in *Again Doctor* when, as the psychiatrist Dr Stoppidge, he tries to discover the secret cure at the slimming clinic by infiltrating it dressed as a very fetching Lady Puddleton. His feminine characteristics are cheekily highlighted in *Doctor* when he suffers a sympathetic pregnancy.

Left: in *Cowboy*, Charles Hawtrey plays an Indian Chief, Big Heap. 'It's one minute peace on, one minute peace off', he comments as he hands the pipe round.

Below: in *Up The Jungle*, he plays Walter, the man who carelessly loses his baby boy – and then himself – while on an expedition in the Jungle.

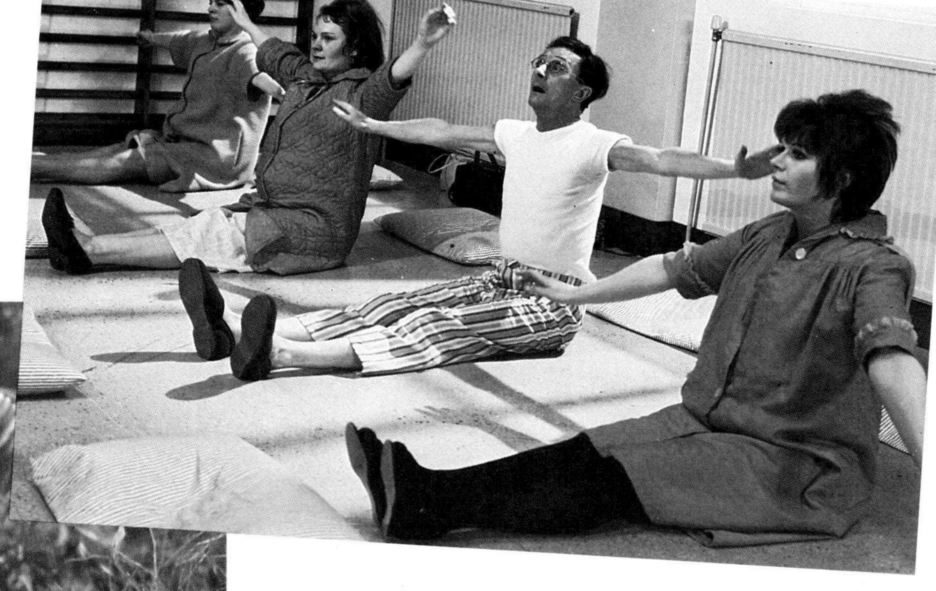

Above: in *Doctor*, he plays Mr Barren who, suffering from a sympathetic pregnancy, has a harder time of it than his wife.

Below left: in *Jack*, Charles Hawtrey plays a cess-pit cleaner, appropriately called Walter Sweetly, who is press-ganged into service for King and Country.

In real life Charles Hawtrey maintains a certain reserve until he knows people well, when he can be extremely garrulous and amusing. He is a keen musician – a brilliant pianist, with a natural ear for a melody, although he never learnt to read music. During the war he was a semi-professional pianist for the Forces and has played in several films. The recordings he made as a boy soprano are sometimes still requested on radio.

He left the Carry Ons in 1972 in poor health, and now lives alone in Deal, Kent.

Carry On Years: 1958–1972 **Carry On Films:** 23

Carry On Titles: Sergeant; Nurse; Teacher; Constable; Regardless; Cabby; Jack; Spying; Cleo; Cowboy; Screaming; Don't Lose Your Head; Follow That Camel; Doctor; Up The Khyber; Again Doctor; Camping; Up The Jungle; Loving; Henry; At Your Convenience; Abroad; Matron.

Carry On Professions: soldier; teacher; special constable; helping hand; taxi driver; cesspool cleaner; sailor; secret agent; prophet; Indian chief; lavatory attendant; French aristocrat; Foreign Legion officer; doctor; tribal king; private detective; courtier; psychiatrist.

Joan Sims, Lady Ruff-Diamond in **Up The Khyber**, hardly saw anything of the beautiful Snowdonia countryside when the film was in production. She suffers from vertigo and kept her eyes shut most of the time. 'I was the only one who sat in a chair **facing** the mountain' she said.

Joan Sims on the set of **Henry**: 'Starting a new Carry On is like going back to school after the hols. My life wouldn't be the same without them.'

Right: Lady Ruff-Diamond (Joan Sims) 'feels a little plastered' as the ceiling collapses around the ears of *Up The Khyber*'s unruffled, very correct English diners, whose opponents have the poor taste to attack their fort during dinner.

Below: Joan plays another gentrified role in *Henry* as Queen Marie who is 'like a bottle of wine that has been left to waste after only one sip', according to King Henry (Sid James).

Below: one of Joan's early Carry On roles was in *Constable* in which she plays the cool, capable and efficient WPC Gloria Passworthy, the only able rookie of a very mixed bunch. Her superior, Sergeant Moon, is the redoubtable Hattie Jacques.

Joan Sims

'Wonderfully talented – one of the best comediennes in the country' is Peter Rogers' description of Joan Sims, a tribute amply borne out by her 24 Carry On films. In true Carry On style, she brings to every role a strong screen personality which is always the same and yet somehow different – and it is the differences which display her remarkable range.

Her buxom figure and mock-refined voice work equally well as the no-nonsense gym mistress who rouses Leslie Phillips' passion in *Teacher*, the nagging, vase-throwing wife in *Screaming* and the nosey-parker mother-in-law in *Behind*. They can also be turned to the more glamorous roles of the haughty, regal beauty in *Henry* and the seductive Madame in *Dick*.

Born in May 1930 in Essex, Joan Sims was a shy and diffident only child – playing out her fantasies by dressing up as other people. She recalls that at an early age she entertained the signalmen and railway passengers alighting at Laindon (where her father was the proud Station Master) mimicking Ginger Rogers, Betty Grable and other film stars of the day.

Her talents were recognized locally when she joined a youth drama group, but she only gained a coveted place at the Royal Academy of Dramatic Art at the fourth attempt. After working in repertory theatre in Manchester and at Salisbury Arts Theatre, and playing Principal Boy in a Glasgow Citizens' Theatre pantomime, she made her West End debut in a revue, *Intimacy at Eight*, at the Irving Theatre. She also had lead roles in several of the Brian Rix farces at the Aldwych Theatre.

Painfully nervous, she sometimes flunked auditions. It was ironic that her first film role, with George Cole in *Will Any Gentleman?* (1953), was offered her by a casting director who had previously turned her down at an audition but had then spotted her afresh in a revue. She has always hated the ordeal of the audition and one of the fruits of success she most values is that she no longer has to do them. 'Nowadays', she told an interviewer, 'they just send for Sims'.

Other screen roles followed, including *Dry Rot* (1956), *Doctor in Love* (1960), *The Belles of St Trinians* (1954) and *The Naked Truth* (1958), but she considers that her film career really took off when she joined the Carry Ons.

Her flair for satirizing lower suburban pretentiousness was quickly revealed in an episode of *Carry On Regardless*. 'Are you a lover of the grape?', asks the pompous organizer of the wine-tasting, for which she has been hired as receptionist. 'Actually, no', she says, in a genteel voice which slides gradually into Cockney, 'I never know what to do with the pips – you know, flick away, collect in the palm of your hand or spit.' Spurning the sips of wine offered her by a snooty official, she insists on glassfuls and becomes outrageously drunk.

This aspect of her screen persona is developed to delicious heights in *Up The Khyber* when, grandly gowned as Lady Ruff-Diamond, wife of the Governor of the North West Province, she presides over the dinner table, ignoring the pounding of the cannons and the chaos all around her, getting quietly and majestically squiffy.

Her portrait of Marie of Normandy, the King's fictitious extra wife in *Henry*, is in a different category. Here, with the naughtiest of French accents, she maintains throughout an unruffled air of commanding regal dignity and unquenchable self-indulgence.

Yet another variation of the Imperial Lady is her performance as Lady Evelyn Bagley, on safari in *Up The Jungle*, whose aristocratic arrogance masks a sexual appetite which she tries to gratify by making condescendingly unsubtle advances to Professor Tinkle (Frankie Howerd). The Professor tells her, 'You remind me of something in an English meadow – a babbling brook'. One would feel so much safer', she says to him nudgingly, 'with a strong, fearless man beside one'. 'Oh, I agree', he replies, 'but where could we find one out here?'

Her relationship with Frankie Howerd, as the charlatan faith healer in *Doctor*, is altogether more downbeat. Her bubbly personality is completely submerged in a dour portrait of a downtrodden, mousy disciple whose claim that he has cured her of deafness is contradicted by the random way she answers his questions. Her one moment of joy is his proposal of marriage – which he only makes because he believes, through a comic misunderstanding, that he is going to die.

Joan Sims is no stranger to loneliness and sadness in real life. Always unsure of herself, even at the height of her success, she has something of the brokenhearted clown within her and is happiest when working full tilt at pretending to be someone else. She has never married – not because she doesn't want to, or indeed, through lack of opportunity, but because the right person has never come along.

She was very close to her mother and also to Hattie

Left: Joan, seen here in *Behind*, is at her comic best with a down-to-earth snobbery when her wonderfully refined characters are outraged by some (usually imagined) slight on her breeding.

Below: Professor Inigo Tinkle (Frankie Howerd) and Lady Evelyn Bagly (Joan Sims) take pleasure in each other's genteel company in *Up The Jungle*.

Sally Geeson in **Abroad**: Of course I already knew Sid James because I'd been his daughter in the TV series **Bless This House**, so in a way he was an introduction to the Carry Ons. But they are all so helpful to anyone new – especially Joan Sims who I found myself turning to for advice, not just about filming but even private things. She's so friendly and such a good listener.

In *Follow That Camel*, Joan plays Zig Zig, 'she who handeth it out on a platter' according to Sheik Abdul Abulbul. Here it is Commandant Burger (Kenneth Williams) who is being offered the dish.

Jacques, who was her dearest friend and helped her through many crises. Dependent on others for self-confidence, she reached a personal low when her mother, Hattie and her long-standing manager and mentor, Peter Eade, all died within a few years of each other. But she can be a tower of strength to other people. Sally Geeson is one of the many who have gained from her friendship and advice.

Her TV work in recent years includes appearances in children's programmes and as a Victorian murderess in an episode of *The Ladykillers*. Viewers will long remember her sparkling performance in the restoration play *The Way of the World*.

Carry On Years: 1959–1978 **Carry On Films:** 24

Carry On Titles: Nurse; Teacher; Constable; Regardless; Cleo; Cowboy; Screaming; Don't Lose Your Head; Follow That Camel; Doctor; Up The Khyber; Again Doctor; Camping; Up The Jungle; Loving; Henry; At Your Convenience; Abroad; Matron; Girls; Dick; Behind; England; Emmannuelle.

Carry On Professions: nurse; gym mistress; policewoman; helping hand; empress; saloon owner; housewife; café proprietress; governor's wife; proprietress of clinic; explorer; queen; factory worker; publican; hotelkeeper; impressario; ATS private; housekeeper.

Barbara Windsor

When Barbara Windsor bubbled into *Carry On Spying*, she brought a new dimension to the series. Romance had been provided first by the coolly glamorous Shirley Eaton and then by the accomplished comedienne Liz Fraser. Barbara's air of cheeky Cockney innocence, contradicted by her scantily clad and seductive shape, exactly fitted the seaside postcard style of Carry On humour.

It was four years and five films before she Carried On again, but when she did she had clearly come to stay. Although she was in less than one-third of the Carry On films, she is justly regarded as a mainstay of the series.

As a trainee secret agent in *Spying*, it is her face and her figure that count, although she wipes the floor with her male colleagues with her photographic brain and her insensitivity to pain. In *Doctor*, her second film of the series, she has little more to do than wriggle her way through the wards and sunbathe in the semi-nude on the hospital roof. But her influence on the action – and on Dr Kilmore (Jim Dale) – is catastrophic. *Camping*, in which she plays a 16-year-old schoolgirl, shows off her assets – when her nightie is accidentally torn off by a fascinated coach driver (Julian Holloway) and when her bra predictably bursts open at a keep fit session on the campsite.

In *Again Doctor* she plays an unexpectedly prim role, refusing Dr Nookie (Dale again) until they are married. Then comes a transformation. She may still look like a dumb blonde, but now the clever side of her screen character, foreshadowed in *Spying*, comes into its own and she emerges as a free-and-equal player of the Carry On games.

Her delightful dewy-eyed naughtiness in *Henry*, in which she plays Bettina, daughter of Lord Bristol (who else?) is tempered by her cunning scheming to marry the King. In *Girls*, as a leather-clad, motorbiking beauty contestant, she has the brains to spring Sid Fiddler (Sid James) from all kinds of trouble. In *Matron*, while it is her appearance which knocks out Kenneth Cope, it is her quick thinking which saves his day.

Left: Barbara Windsor is at her cheekiest in *Henry*. As Bettina, daughter of the Earl of Bristol (predictably), she tells the amorous King (Sid James), 'I promised my mother I'd be a good Bet'.

Right: in *Again Doctor*, she plays the appropriately named Goldie Locks, a model who ends up in hospital when filming an advert for Bristol's bouncing baby food. Goldie's real name is Maud Boggins.

Below: Chayste Place is a school for young ladies which has difficulty living up to its name when Barbara Windsor becomes one of the pupils.

When Barbara Windsor married Ronnie Knight they went to Madeira for their honeymoon. 'I'll come with you' volunteered Kenneth Williams – and he did. What's more, his mother and sister came too.

Above: Barbara was in three of the hospital-based Carry Ons, but only twice played a nurse. In *Doctor*, she is introduced to Dr Kilmore (Jim Dale), a nervous, jumpy medic who is continually bumping into things. He cannot believe his eyes when he first takes stock of Nurse May.

Right: Barbara's debut with the Carry On team was in *Spying*, in which she plays special agent Daphne Honeybutt (code name: Brown Cow), the cream of the new intake. Despite appearances to the contrary, she is here being measured for her holster by special agent Howard Crump (Bernard Cribbins).

Above: Barbara is often put into a position where her assets are (nearly) on full public display. In *Camping* (left), it is during morning exercises while in *Abroad* she is surprised by Vic Flange (Sid James).

Camping was the first of many occasions on which she played opposite Sid James. In *Henry*, the screen flirtation continues: 'My mother says I must save myself until I have a husband', she coyly tells the King. 'Well that's all right', he replies, 'I am a husband'. 'That's right – so you are, aren't you?' she giggles, her sexy laugh matching Sid James's chortle for earthiness. In *Dick*, her last Carry On, she played two roles, a most unlikely highwayman (more akin to a principal boy) and a fetching serving-wench, both in the service of Sid James as Dick Turpin/Reverend Flasher. In 1977 she did the commentary, with Kenneth Williams, for *That's Carry On*.

Barbara was born in 1937 in Shoreditch, where her father was a bus conductor and her mother a dressmaker. She was a bright pupil at school, and her parents wanted her to go to university, but her first taste of showbiz – an appearance in a dance-school show – convinced her that her future lay on the stage. She was invited to take part in a local pantomime, but the school authorities disapproved of the time-off needed for rehearsals, and she was eventually asked to leave. Her mother spent her savings on a place at the Ada Foster acting school, where the tutors misguidedly tried to iron out her Cockney accent. Luckily Joan Littlewood, the producer whose commitment to working-class theatre transformed the London stage, spotted Barbara at an audition and gave her the role which changed her life – the perky Rosie in *Fings Ain't What They Used To Be*. She appeared in Littlewood's stage version of *Oh! What a Lovely War* and toured the United States with it.

She made her screen debut in *The Belles of St Trinians* (1954), playing a leggy schoolgirl. She had several other roles before getting the lead in Littlewood's high-spirited East End comedy, *Sparrows Can't Sing* (1963). It was in this film that she was spotted by Peter Rogers and offered the roles which established her as a talented comedy actress. Her TV work includes a lead part in the third series of *The Rag Trade* and appearances in *Dad's Army*, *Up Pompeii!* and *The Des O'Connor Show*.

Her career has gone from strength to strength on the stage, in TV and in cabaret where her act includes songs, dances and mimicry. Barbara says that her biggest professional regret is that they only wanted unknown faces in TV's *EastEnders*.

Carry On Years: 1964–1974 **Carry On Films:** 9

Carry On Titles: Spying; Doctor; Again Doctor; Camping; Henry; Abroad; Matron; Girls; Dick.

Carry On Professions: secret agent; nurse; dancer; schoolgirl; lady-in-waiting; beauty contestant; highwayman; serving wench.

Kenneth Connor

When Kenneth Connor is playing in a comedy run, he sometimes yearns to be involved in a more serious classical role. And when he is playing Shakespeare or modern drama, he often feels an inescapable longing for the fun and games of the comedy show.

'I have what is almost a need,' he says, 'to balance comedy with drama'. It is this two-way pull which gives his Carry On characterisations their surprising depth. Inside many of his funny little men is a serious little man struggling to be given voice.

Typically, in the early Carry On films, he is a nervous little chap lusting after a woman who appears unattainable, or so obsessed with his own shortcomings that he fails to notice the woman who is lusting after **him**. Then, rather like Popeye with his spinach, something happens which transforms him into an indomitable go-getter. His chest puffs out and he's away.

As Horace Strong, one of the rookies in *Carry On Sergeant*, he is too absorbed in his own imaginary illnesses to notice that one of the NAAFI girls (Dora Bryan) is madly in love with him. It is only after Hattie Jacques, as the Company MO, has called his bluff by putting him through every medical test in the book, and tired him out so that he falls asleep dreaming of Doris, that he changes his character and not only wins the girl but also becomes a model soldier.

As a science master in *Teacher*, he is so nervous of declaring his love for the formidable inspector Miss Wheeler (Rosemary Knight) that his words come out every which way but in the right order.

In *Cruising*, as an accident-prone ship's medical officer, he dare not reveal his love for the husband-hunting Dilys Laye, but serenades her anonymously with a song and a guitar.

Although Connor's Carry On career spans the whole series from *Sergeant* to *Emmannuelle*, he was absent from several in the middle. However, this period features his most outstanding portrayal, that of Hengist Pod, the henpecked Ancient British cave-dweller who invents the square wheel in *Cleo*. He is captured by the Romans and

Kenneth Connor affectionately recalls an incident during the shooting of **Carry On Nurse**. His son Jeremy, then aged 3½, had a tiny role, greeting his father as he left hospital. Director Gerald Thomas was pleased with the first take. 'That was very good, Jeremy' he said, 'but now we need to do it again' and he explained the need for an 'insurance shot'. When the little boy seemed reluctant, Gerald offered him a box of bricks if he would comply. He went through the scene again, with no faults. 'Now,' said the young Jeremy, 'where's me bloody bricks?'

Above: Kenneth as one of the Bow Street Runners in *Dick*, the last 'costume' Carry On.

Left: in *Cleo*, Kenneth Connor plays Hengist, the ancient Briton who lists the invention of the square wheel amongst his achievements. He is also a rank coward, which causes problems when he finds himself assigned to Caesar (Kenneth Williams) as his supposedly fearless bodyguard.

Right: *Cruising* sees Kenneth playing the smooth but excitable Dr Binn, here taking his morning constitutional with one of the oldest passengers (Esma Cannon). It was a typical role for him in the early days of the Carry Ons.

winds up, through a case of mistaken identity, as Julius Caesar's bodyguard. His Popeye-like transformation occurs when, replacing the cowardly Caesar in Cleopatra's bedroom, he drinks some of her love potion. This not only achieves wonders in Egypt but also transforms his relationship with his wife Senna (Sheila Hancock) when he returns to their cave. His sensitive portrayal of the dreamy, innocent Hengist is a remarkable comic creation.

In his later *Carry On* roles, he plays an altogether more ineffectual character whose manhood is permanently impaired: the major who continually loses face or his trousers in *Girls*, or the forever expectant father, worn out in the waiting-room in *Matron*. His Major Leep, the caravan-site owner in *Behind*, is virtually a straight characterisation, but he returned to broad comedy as the hapless Captain S Melly in *England* and the leery chauffeur, Leyland, in *Emmannuelle*.

Several of the Carry On regulars began their show-business careers at an early age, but Connor was the earliest starter of them all. Born in London in June 1918, his first appearance on stage was at the tender age of two, in Portsmouth, where his father, a petty officer on the Royal

Yacht *Victoria and Albert*, was helping to set up service concerts for charity. 'I've got a photograph to prove it', he says, 'it shows a bunch of chaps dressed as black and white minstrels, my mother with a money box, my father with a banjo and me perched on top of the barrel organ'. His father taught Kenneth and his brother basic steps and songs and they continued to appear in concerts throughout childhood.

When his father left the Navy to run a pub, Kenneth served behind the bar and took drama lessons in his spare time. In 1933 he gained a place at the Central School of Speech and Drama and was a gold medal winner in his final year. His first professional engagement was in J M Barrie's *The Boy David*, in 1936. He made his film debut three years later.

After wartime service in the Middlesex Regiment, he toured the Middle East with Stars in Battledress, and became a close friend of fellow-actor William Devlin, whose pre-war King Lear had been highly acclaimed. Devlin became his life-line to the post-war theatrical scene. While waiting to be demobbed in Cairo, Connor received a cable from Devlin asking him to join him at the newly-formed Bristol Old Vic. After what Kenneth describes as 'the slowest boat journey on record', he arrived for rehearsals at a London theatre and was on the stage before he had time to remove his boots and gaiters. He looks back on his three years at Bristol, playing classic drama and modern plays, as one of the most satisfying periods in his stage career.

Left: as Captain Melly in *England*, Kenneth Connor is sent to command an experimental mixed battery during the Second World War. By the end of the film, victory is – just – his.

Above: in *Teacher*, he plays the archetypal absent-minded professor – the chemistry teacher Mr Adams who can rarely get his sentences out in the right order.

Above right: in *Girls*, Kenneth Connor shambles on as Mayor Frederick Bumble, an apt title for the ineffectual politician.

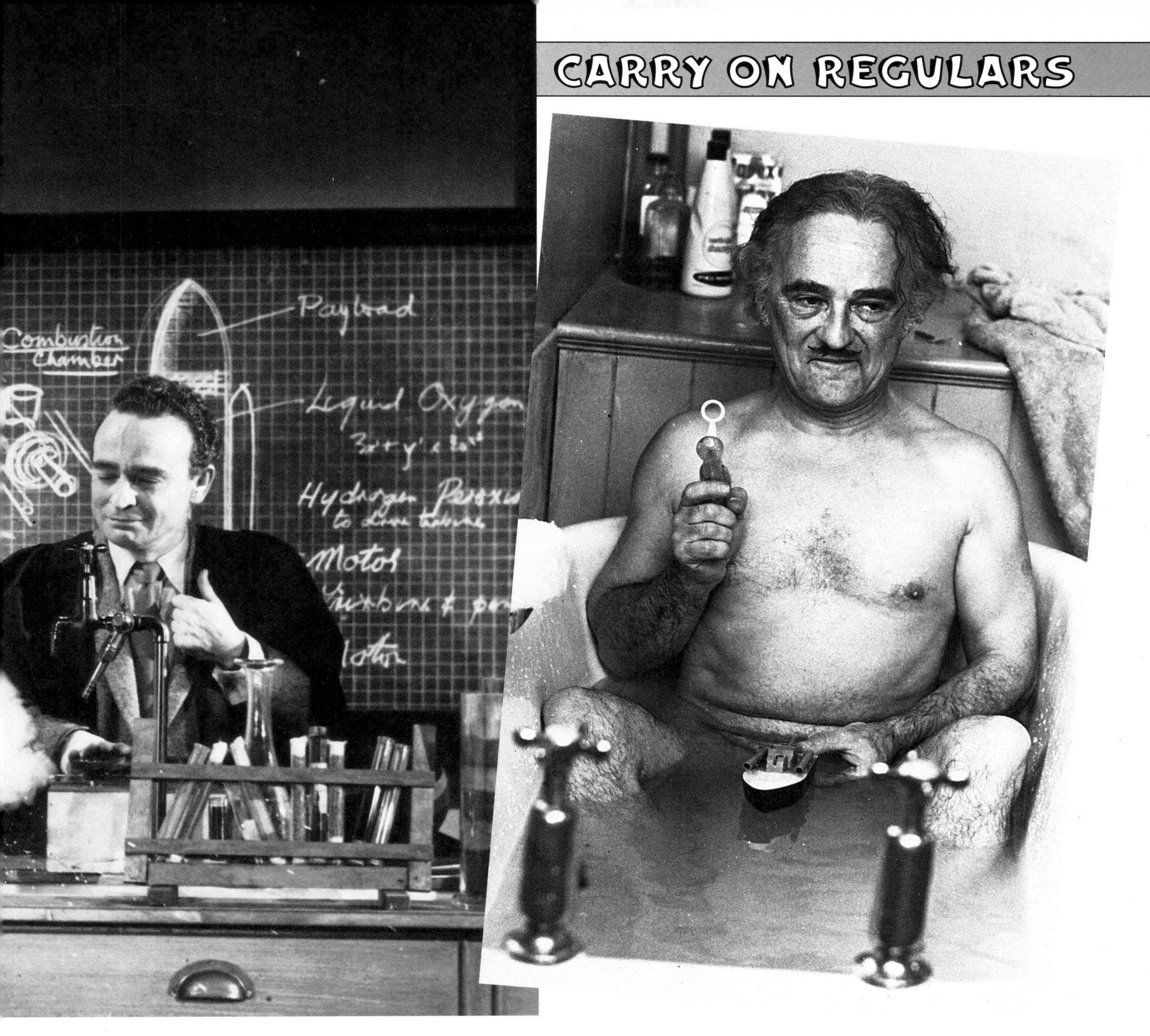

The two-way pull, however, took him back to comedy. Drawn to radio work, he became something of a household name to listeners in his eleven years with Ted Ray in *Ray's A Laugh*, with Jack Warner and Kathleen Harrison in *Meet the Huggetts* and with Eric Barker in *Just Fancy*. At the same time he appeared in several Shakespearean roles on TV.

His association with the Carry Ons, from 1958 onwards, was a watershed in his career. 'Like a cork on an ocean of joy', is how he describes it. It led to further film and stage comedy roles, including a key role in the West End stage version of *A Funny Thing Happened on the Way to the Forum*, with Frankie Howerd in the lead. He took over direction of the show when it went on tour, with fellow Carry On veteran Charles Hawtrey filling his West End role.

His career took another step foward when he began appearing in the popular TV comedies *Hi-de-hi* and *'Allo, 'Allo*.

Kenneth never watches his own work when it appears on TV. 'What's done is done,' he says, 'and on with the next'. But there's one Carry On he always watches out for – *Carry On Nurse*. It's like a family movie to him. It's not his own performance he's interested in but that of his son, Jeremy, then aged three-and-a-half, who comes in at the end to greet his screen and real-life Daddy when he leaves hospital. Jeremy appears with him again, years later, in *Dick, Behind* and *England*.

At home Kenneth enjoys reading books about the sea and has a boat on the Thames. He is a keen football fan. His wife, Margaret, describes him as 'a very private person who shuns publicity'. But on the set his witty asides make him a very popular member of the team. 'If I had to be locked up', Sid James once said, 'Kenneth would be one of my choices for cell-mate'.

Carry On Years: 1958–1978 **Carry On Films:** 17

Carry On Titles: Sergeant; Nurse; Teacher; Constable; Regardless; Cruising; Cabby; Cleo; Up The Jungle; Henry; Abroad; Matron; Girls; Dick; Behind; England; Emmannuelle.

Carry On Professions: soldier; boxer; teacher; policeman; helping hand; ship's doctor; taxi driver; ancient British wheelwright; bodyguard; ornithologist; courtier; businessman; railwayman; mayor; Bow Street runner; holiday camp owner; army officer; chauffeur.

Jim Dale

Singer, songwriter, composer, stand-up comic, DJ, actor on stage and screen in everything from musical comedy to Shakespearean tragedy – Jim Dale has done it all. And having done it all in England, he went to the United States to do it all over again.

In between hosting TV's *6.5 Special* and acting in Shakespeare at the Old Vic, he found time for ten Carry On films in six years. His cheeky good looks and boyish demeanour enabled him to project the personality of a naive folktale character – a kind of Careless Jim who does all the wrong things but wins out in the end.

His early Carry On roles were really bit parts. His first appearance, as the nerve-racked expectant father in *Cabby*, is a highly effective cameo. In *Jack* he appears as a straw-chewing country-bumpkin, complete with West Country accent and peasant cunning, as he hoodwinks the gentlemanly fool of a midshipman (Bernard Cribbins) into paying for services unrendered. In *Spying*, as Our Man in Vienna, he displays his versatility by popping up at street corners in an endless variety of disguises. At this point, he became a fully-fledged Carry On-er with a specific role to play.

In the earliest Carry Ons, Terence Longden filled the romantic male role in straight matinée idol style. Bernard Cribbins had two bites at the cherry. Then Jim Dale took over the romantic mantle in films like *Doctor* (with Barbara Windsor), *Screaming* and *Cowboy* (both with Angela Douglas). His bashful, bumbling innocence became an essential ingredient in Carry On comedy. In *Screaming*, Sergeant Bung is trying to identify the exact spot in the woods where Jim's girlfriend disappeared. 'You took her into the woods', he says. 'How far did you go?' 'Not very far', Jim replies modestly, ''cos I've only known her for a year'.

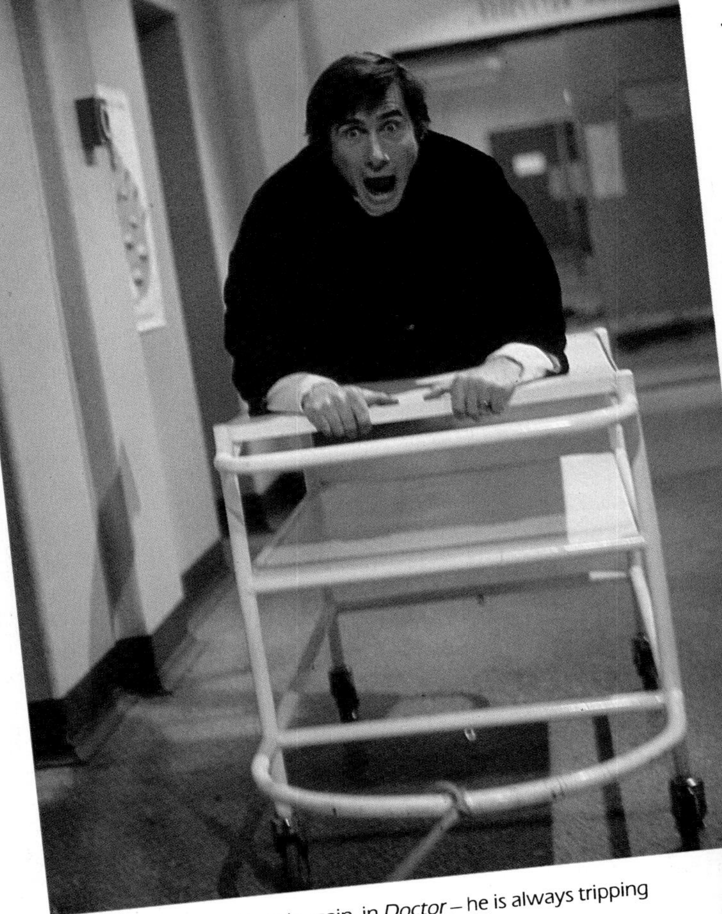

Dr Kilmore (Jim Dale) is at it again, in *Doctor* – he is always tripping up at the wrong moments.

Right: in *Screaming*, gentlemanly Albert Potter (Jim Dale) protects his girlfriend (Angela Douglas) from prying eyes even when she has been turned into a shop dummy.

Below: a spell in the Beatific Isles is enough to drive anyone to jigsaws; even the amorous Dr Nookey (Jim Dale) can find nothing better to do in *Again Doctor*.

Below right: Jim Dale turned in a lovely cameo as the local yokel with his sedan chair in *Jack*, one of his early Carry Ons.

When Jim Dale left the series the rest of the regulars felt that he had let them down and were so upset that they refused to take part in his projected **This Is Your Life.**

Above: Bo West (Jim Dale), the very proper and correct English gentleman of *Follow That Camel*, finds that clearing his name is not as easy as falling off a camel when he tries to join the Foreign Legion.

Left: Jim, as the bungling Dr Kilmore in *Doctor*, gets into all the wrong places.

Opposite: (from left to right) Sheriff Albert Earp (Jon Pertwee), Judge Burke (Kenneth Williams) and Marshall P. Knutt (Jim Dale) try to bolster each other's courage in the face of the scourge of Stodge City, the Rumpo Kid.

His role in *Cowboy*, as the sanitary engineer Marshall P Knutt, is one of the high points of his Carry On career. In his eagerness to clean up Stodge City's drains, he fails to notice that everyone is treating him with greater respect than is warranted by his humble position. The good citizens believe him to be the peace officer who has been despatched to clean up their town by restoring law and order. When the penny drops, Dale sustains that wonderfully dithering ambivalence which is his stock in trade – eager to be a hero, yet anxious to pursue his professional enthusiasm for water-pipes; yearning to impress Annie Oakley (Angela Douglas) with his bravery, yet fearing for his life.

He falls for Angela Douglas again in *Follow That Camel*, in which he has a more gentlemanly role, as the upper-class Bo West who is unjustly dishonoured on the cricket field and joins the Foreign Legion to clear his name. Typically it is innocence rather than guile, ignorance rather than tactics, which enable him to save the garrison.

He had a very different role in *Carry On Cleo*, as the dashing Ancient Briton Horsa, a fearless fighter of Romans and legendary swordsman. This time his courage and bravery are thwarted by circumstances and he fails to receive the honours which are his due.

His roles in *Doctor* and *Again Doctor* resemble each other. In both he is a hapless, accident-prone medic who falls victim to the jealousies and machinations of the hospital hierarchy. Through coincidence, luck and the occasional spark of quick thinking, he managed to win the day – and get the girl (Barbara Windsor in both cases).

Dale was hooked on show business while still at school, taking dancing lessons in his spare time. While working at a shoe factory, he was chosen as one of *Carol Levis's Discoveries* (a TV forerunner of talent shows like *New Faces*) and worked as a teenage stand-up comic. He began to make a name for himself as a pop singer and TV personality, and his hosting of *6.5 Special* brought him instant fame. It was in 1966, the year of *Carry On Screaming*, that he made his Shakespearean debut – as Autolycus in *A Winter's Tale*, a highly-acclaimed Edinburgh Festival and London production which was later made into a film. He wrote the music for the Shakespeare songs.

Among his other songwriting successes of the late 1960s were the lyrics for the title song of the hit film *Georgy Girl* (1966), which was nominated for an Academy Award; the lyrics for the songs in the film *Shalako* (1968); and all the songs for *Twinky* (1969). His own recording of 'Be My Girl' reached No 2 in the charts.

Among his first feature films were *The Iron Maiden* (1962) and *Raising the Wind* (1961). As these were both produced by Peter Rogers and directed by Gerald Thomas, they led naturally to the Carry Ons. While he was working on *Doctor* he had a heavy schedule – he was appearing on stage in the evening in the pop version of *A Midsummer Night's Dream* at the Saville Theatre – a production which had originated at the 1967 Edinburgh Festival.

His work with the Pop Theatre Group, forerunner of the Young Vic, led to the lead role in the National Theatre production of Peter Barnes's *The National Health* (1970). His performance was highly praised both in the stage production and the film version. Other notable film roles were in *Digby – The Biggest Dog in the World* and *Adolph Hitler – My Part in His Downfall* (both 1973).

A change of direction came when, after playing many roles at the Young Vic, he took the physically demanding lead in *Scapino*, which he helped to adapt from the Molière original. *Scapino* was a major success in Los Angeles, San Francisco and on Broadway and earned Dale the Drama Desk Award and the Outer Critics' Circle Award.

A wide variety of offers poured in. He settled in the United States and chose a Disney Studio option, playing one of the medicine men in *Pete's Dragon* (1977) and the dastardly Sir Mordred in *The Spacemen and King Arthur* (1979). In *Bloodshy* (1979) he took three roles – twins and their aged father. As in *Scapino*, this was an energetic assignment, bringing Jim's athleticism fully into play. He did all his own stunts and was given the rare distinction of honorary membership of the Association of Hollywood stuntmen.

His most recent Broadway successes include lead roles in the hugely successful *Barnum* and *Me and My Girl*. 'I've done it all in Britain', he told a reporter, 'it's just lovely to surprise people here, all over again'.

Carry On Years: 1963–1969 **Carry On Films:** 10

Carry On Titles: Cabby; Jack; Spying; Cleo; Cowboy; Screaming; Don't Lose Your Head; Follow That Camel; Doctor; Again Doctor.

Carry On Professions: carrier; secret agent; galley slave; sanitary engineer; law marshal; aristocrat; legionnaire; doctor; surgeon; proprietor of a clinic.

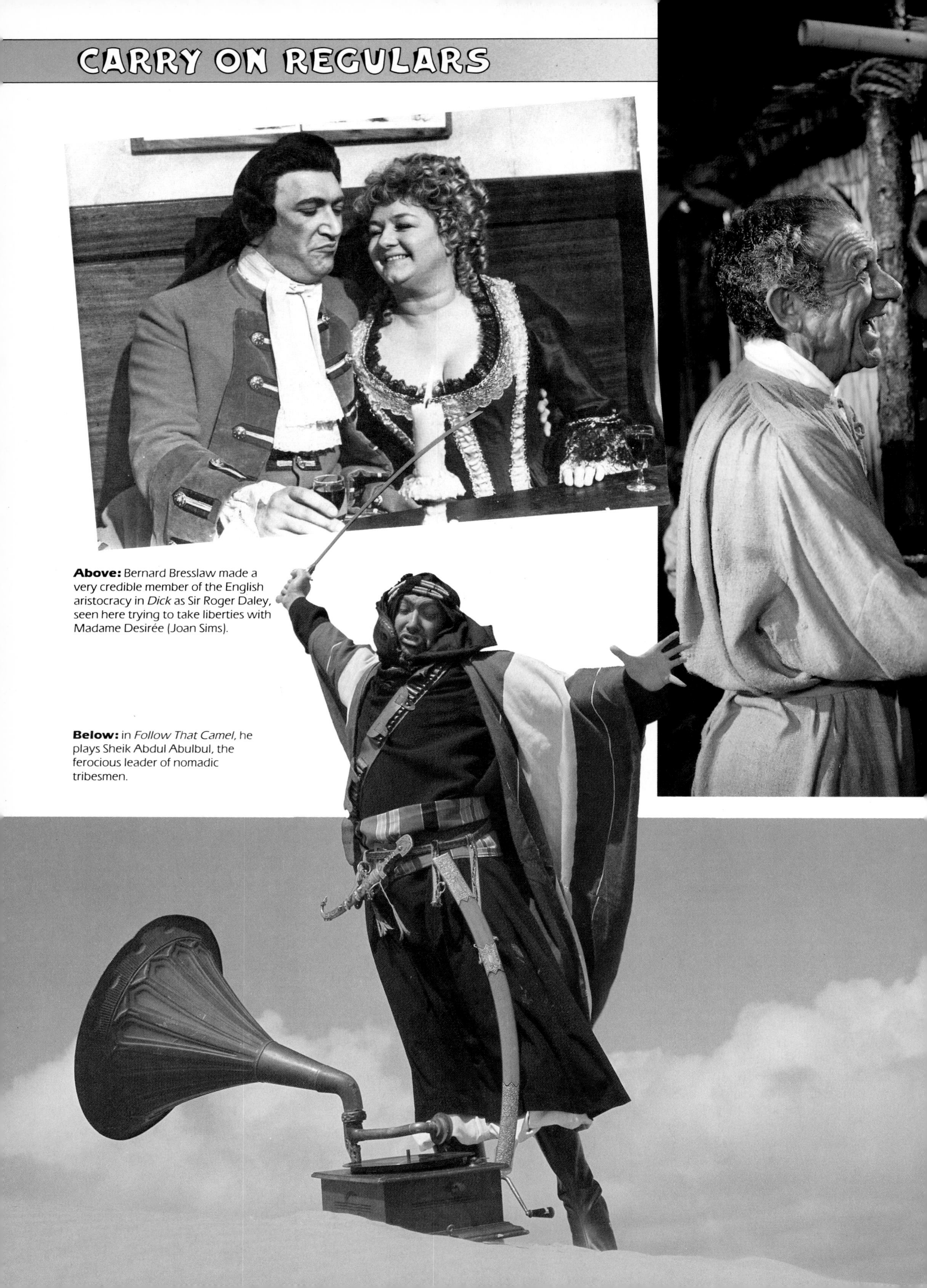

Above: Bernard Bresslaw made a very credible member of the English aristocracy in *Dick* as Sir Roger Daley, seen here trying to take liberties with Madame Desirée (Joan Sims).

Below: in *Follow That Camel*, he plays Sheik Abdul Abulbul, the ferocious leader of nomadic tribesmen.

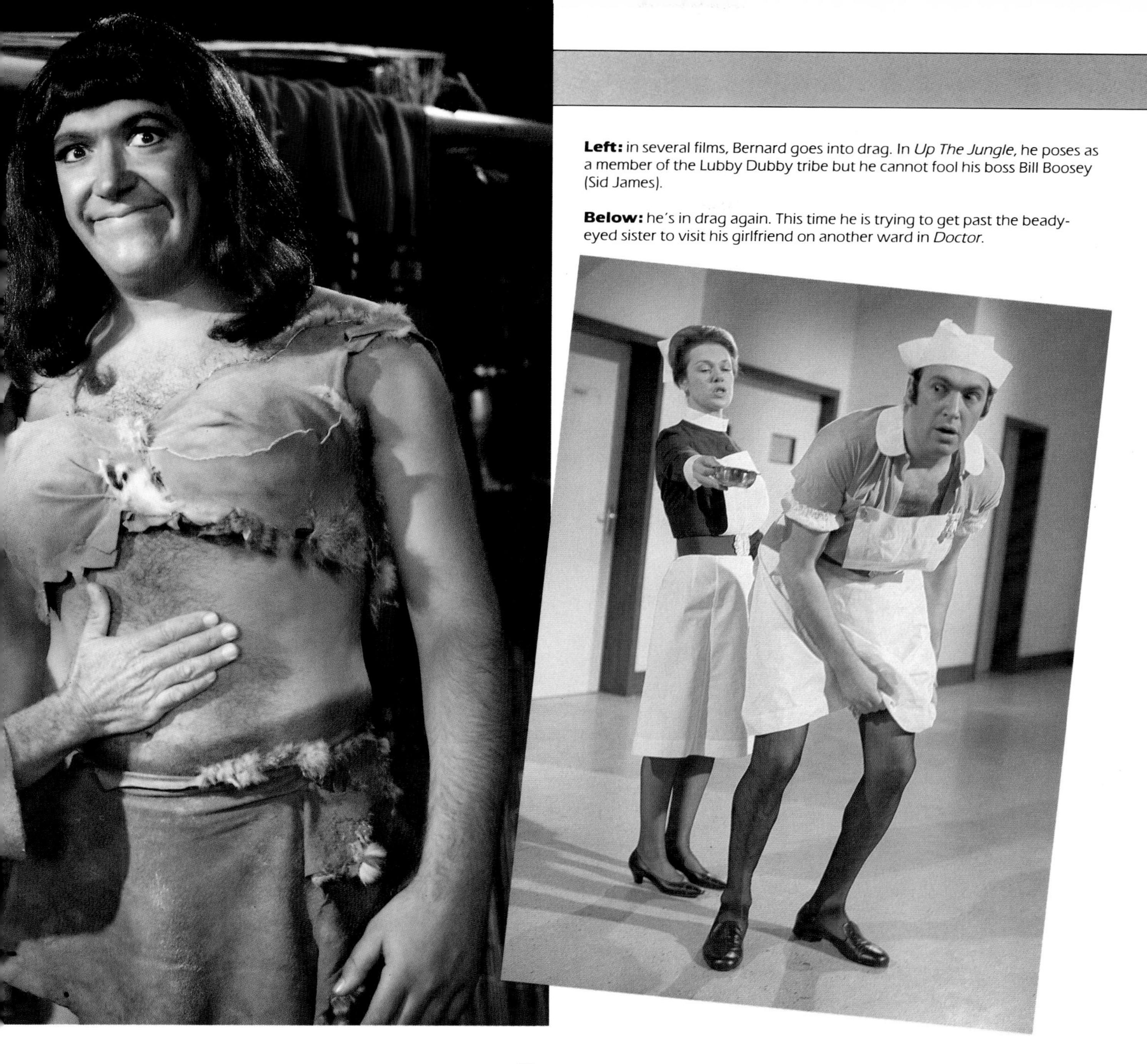

Left: in several films, Bernard goes into drag. In *Up The Jungle,* he poses as a member of the Lubby Dubby tribe but he cannot fool his boss Bill Boosey (Sid James).

Below: he's in drag again. This time he is trying to get past the beady-eyed sister to visit his girlfriend on another ward in *Doctor.*

Bernard Bresslaw

At 6ft 7in Bernard Bresslaw is by far the tallest of the Carry On regulars: he stands a good head above Kenneth Connor (5ft 5in) and a solid head and shoulders above Barbara Windsor (4ft 10in).

When he decided at an early age to take up acting, he thought his height would be a disadvantage. But it has served him well, winning him his first stage role when Laurence Olivier was looking for someone to play an Irish wrestler for his production of *The MacRoary Whirl*. And the Carry Ons have always made the most of his stature.

In *Cowboy*, his first Carry On, he is ironically cast as the aggressive Indian Little Heap, towering over his father (Charles Hawtrey) the peaceloving Indian Chief, Big Heap. In *Screaming*, he plays the lurching, inscrutable butler Sockett. In *Follow That Camel* he dominates the desert as the powerful Sheik Abdul Abulbul whose portentous sayings include 'the behaviour of the white infidel is like blood coming from a stone – a bleeding mystery'. In *Up The Khyber* he makes a proud and awesome Burpa tribal leader, Bungdit Dinn. In the midst of his attack on the British residency, he flings a personal hand grenade over the ramparts. 'That'll teach 'em', he cries jubilantly, 'to ban turbans on the buses'.

In *Loving*, he excels as the insanely jealous prize wrestler Gripper Burke, whose sudden appearance in the bedroom of his girlfriend (Joan Sims) frightens the life out of her would-be lover, Sid James.

However, there is much more to his Carry On performances than bone and brawn. There is no one quite like Bernard for expressing, in a variety of carefully thought-out characterizations, the gormless bewilderment of an innocent caught up in someone else's manoeuvres. In *Camping* Sid (Sid James), invites him to share in his scheme for luring their two girlfriends, Joan Sims and Dilys Laye, into what he believes to be a nudist camp. The conflict between his loyalty to Sid and his respect for the girls can be read all over his face. There is a gentle-giant tenderness in his romance with Dilys Laye (also pursued in the earlier *Doctor*), and a great deal of charm in the contrast between his big frame and her petite figure.

Another engaging romance emerges from his portrayal of Brother Bernard, on holiday with a group of fellow monks in *Abroad*, who finds worldly temptations hard to resist and shows a far from brotherly interest in Lily (Sally Geeson).

His size makes him an especially amusing exponent of the art of drag – a staple ploy of Carry On films. As a beauty contest publicist in *Girls* he ends up, in a publicity stunt, as a hulking contestant. A member of the pill-thieving gang in *Matron*, he gatecrashes the maternity hospital as an expectant mother, his voluminous summer dress concealing his burglary gear, and leaves nursing a blanketed bundle in which the loot is hidden.

Bresslaw was born in 1934 in the heart of London's East End, and he remains proud of the route – and the talent – which took him from a working-class upbringing to the heights of his profession. 'I am the son of a poor East End tailor's cutter', he says, recalling the first fruits of celebrity. 'I had seen my mother forced to take in sewing to help with the household bills and it made me feel good to be in a position to help them'.

At school he was encouraged by his English teacher and won two of the annual London County Council awards to the Royal Academy of Dramatic Art, where he gained the coveted Emile Littler award for the most promising actor. For a time he toured small venues – army camps, prisons and hospitals – playing the lead in *The Hasty Heart*. His London debut, as juvenile lead in *Bachelor's Honeymoon*, was a disaster. It opened on a Thursday and closed on the Saturday. 'For a while', he says, 'it held the record as the shortest run ever'.

He made his first big impact on the general public as Sergeant Popplewell, the gawky, thick-headed 'Popeye' in the original TV *Army Game* series, which ran from 1957-1958. It was during this period that he also gained fame as a recording artiste when his 'Mad Pashernate Love', originally recorded as a joke, reached No. 4 in the UK charts, with a Max Bygraves take-off, 'You Need Feet', on the flip side.

For a time his Popeye personality, and his plaintive catchphrase 'I only arsked' were so well-known that they were something of an embarrassment (although he cheerfully uses the expression as Sid James' foil in several Carry Ons). He was acutely aware of the perils of typecasting. After refusing a number of roles in the Popeye mould, he went through a depressing period when, as he recalls, 'the phone stopped ringing altogether'. Eventually he went where his heart led him – to the Regent's Park Open Air Theatre, playing in a variety of Shakespearean roles and winning the Variety Club of Great Britain's Most Promising Newcomer Award.

Bresslaw is as much at home in the classics as in broad comedy. His dramatic credits include Quince in *A Midsummer Night's Dream* with Frank Dunlop's Company; the professor in Ionesco's *The Lesson*; a 16th-century monk in *Rabelais*, at the Round House, directed by the great French actor Jean-Louis Barrault; and the lead role in the Old Vic's production of *Oblomov*.

One of the turning points in his career came with a part in TV's *Z Cars*. But it was his work with the Carry Ons which re-established him as one of Britain's foremost comedy actors.

In addition to his Carry Ons, he has appeared in many

Above: in *At Your Convenience*, even Bernie (played by Bernie) occasionally has difficulty suffering the plans of his mate, Vic Spanner (Kenneth Cope).

Right: as Brother Bernard in *Abroad*, he plays a highly unlikely and ultimately unreligious member of the holy orders.

Below: in *Girls*, when someone is needed to add some colour to the local beauty competition, who should they look for but Peter Potter (Bernard), who makes a lovely girl, even in his underwear.

other films including *Morgan: A Suitable Case for Treatment* (1966); *Up Pompeii!* (1971) and *One of Our Dinosaurs is Missing* (1975). Like many of the other Carry On artistes, he is a regular in pantomime.

A real-life gentle giant, Bresslaw is a quiet and studious man who takes a great delight in his family – his wife, Liz, and their three sons – but also enjoys withdrawing into his study for a good read.

Carry On Years: 1965–1975 **Carry On Films:** 14

Carry On Titles: Cowboy; Screaming; Follow That Camel; Doctor; Up The Khyber; Camping; Up The Jungle; Loving; At Your Convenience; Abroad; Matron; Girls; Dick; Behind.

Carry On Professions: Indian brave; butler; sheik; Indian tribal leader; tracker; wrestler; factory worker; monk; petty thief; publicist; Bow Street runner.

Terry Scott

Left: in *Up The Jungle*, Terry Scott had a stab at the Tarzan figure – but a Carry On jungle boy is forever bumping into trees and missing his creepers.

Right: two schemers at the court of the English king – Cromwell, the plotting Chancellor, is played by Kenneth Williams while Terry Scott takes the part of the more pious Cardinal Wolsey.

Below: no wonder the Third Foot and Mouth, the regimental heroes of *Up The Khyber*, are in trouble when they have to rely on equipment like this. Terry Scott plays Sergeant Major MacNutt and Charles Hawtrey, Private Widdle.

Terry Scott had a small role as Sergeant O'Brien in *Carry On Sergeant* but didn't turn up again until *Up The Khyber*, one rung up the army ladder as Sergeant-Major MacNutt of the Third Foot and Mouth Regiment – a blustering character which marked him out as a true Carrier On.

The put-upon husband in *Camping*, the wife-seeker in *Loving* and the lecherous Dr. Prodd in *Matron* are variations on the theme of Suburban Man, for which he is best known on stage and TV. *Up The Khyber* and his two subsequent 'historicals' gave him a chance to display a wider range of comic invention and to demonstrate his amazing way with facial expressions. As Jungle Boy in *Up The Jungle* he is a big, plump, baby-faced Tarzan who can't swing on a rope without bumping into a tree but who proves to be a wide-eyed, eager pupil when June (Angela Douglas) gives him an elementary lesson on the differences between the sexes. You can almost see his brain ticking over as he cottons on to the potential of his new-found knowledge.

His Cardinal Wolsey in *Henry* is a slow-witted prelate, hard put to grasp the machinations of his fellow courtiers. His plump, round face goes through the gamut of anguished expressions as Queen Marie, relying on him to smuggle out a secret letter from the dungeon in which she is incarcerated, explains the bodily places in which he could hide it.

'Fire at will' . . . 'Poor old Will, wh
do they always pick on him'.

Terry Scott on the set of **Henry:** 'Playing Cardinal Wolsey left me with one burning ambition unfulfilled. Every time I got into the splendid red robes of the Cardinal I had an irresistible urge to sneak them out of the studio and wear them to my local church on Sunday morning. Mind you I wouldn't have made a big thing of it – just sat in the back row and watched the vicar's reaction.'

Born in Watford, Scott studied accountancy, served in the Navy during World War II and afterwards used his gratuity to break into showbusiness. After a gruelling period of touring pubs and clubs and a spell teamed up with Bill Maynard – *Great Scott, It's Maynard* and others – he was invited by Brian Rix to play in a series of Whitehall farces. From then on his career took wings.

His work with Hugh Lloyd in the *Hugh and I* TV series led to his own TV shows, *Scott on Habit*, *Scott on Marriage*, *Scott On . . .* various other subjects and thence to his partnership with June Whitfield in the most popular of all his TV series, *Terry and June*.

Constantly busy with TV, pantomimes, summer shows, tours and West End farce, even, sometimes, to the point of exhaustion, Scott hasn't always been available for filming. But that's the only reason he has ever turned down a Carry On offer. 'I would never for a moment,' he says, 'think of saying "No more Carry Ons".'

Carry On Years: 1958–1972 **Carry On Films:** 7

Carry On Titles: Sergeant; Up The Khyber; Camping; Up The Jungle; Loving; Henry; Matron.

Carry On Professions: army sergeant; army sergeant-major; businessman; jungle dweller; cardinal; doctor.

Patsy Rowlands

With her dumpy figure, woebegone face and tearfully expressive eyes, Patsy Rowlands has carved a niche for herself in nine Carry Ons as the hard-done-by wife or the put-upon employee. But she is no mere ugly duckling for there is always a twist that motivates her to turn herself into a swan. In *Loving*, she plays the lovelorn housekeeper Miss Dempsey, suppressing her passion for her employer (Kenneth Williams) until competition (in the shape of Hattie Jacques) forces her to reveal her hidden assets. Although she has a hard time testing loos at Boggs Sanitary Ware factory in *At Your Convenience*, she is transformed under pressure, and finally captures her initially unwilling boss (Williams, again). In the film she delivers the memorable line: 'I've given my whole life to Boggs'.

She is glimpsed only briefly in *Henry* – she's the unfortunate queen who is topped at the beginning of the film to make bedroom for Marie of Normandy (Joan Sims). But she comes into her own in *Behind*, as the long-suffering Linda Upmore, sharing a caravan with her roving-eyed husband (Bernard Bresslaw), her interfering mother (Joan Sims) and a foulmouthed mynah bird.

Outstanding among her Carry On roles is her portrayal of Mildred Bumble, the slovenly wife of the mayor (Kenneth Connor) in *Girls*. Reduced to total apathy by her boring,

Below: in *Again Doctor*, she follows Gladstone Screwer half way across the world to the Beatific Islands.

One of the delights of Patsy Rowlands' characterizations in the Carry On films is her transformations. **Above:** in *Girls*, she is the bored, sluttish wife of the Mayor (Kenneth Williams) – an ugly duckling; while **left** in *Loving*, she is the housekeeper of Percival Snooper (Kenneth Williams) – a swan.

incompetent and self-important husband, she slouches around the house in her dressing-gown and disgraces him at public functions. But, finally, in a mood of glorious rebellion, she sheds her downtrodden image, joins the Women's Libbers and plays a sterling part in sabotaging the beauty queen competition.

Born in 1934, she attended a succession of convent schools without any sense of direction until a new elocution teacher, recognizing her potential, encouraged her to apply for a Guildhall School of Speech and Drama scholarship. She won it when she was just 15, coming top in the whole of England. She spent several years at the Players' Theatre in London and was very much a part of the 'new wave' which brought a fresh and exciting mood to stage and screen in the late Fifties and early Sixties. She appeared in plays like N F Simpson's bizarre comedy *One-Way Pendulum* and in *Semi-Detached*, directed by Tony Richardson and starring Laurence Olivier. It was in Richardson's *Tom Jones* (1963) that she made her film debut.

A wide range of comedy and straight roles have made her a familiar figure to TV viewers, especially her portrayal of Betty, the feckless neighbour in the popular sit-com *Bless This House*, which starred fellow Carry On-er Sid James.

Carry On Years: 1969–1975 **Carry On Films:** 9

Carry On Titles: Again Doctor; Loving; Henry; At Your Convenience; Abroad; Matron; Girls; Dick; Behind.

Carry On Professions: housekeeper; queen; loo-tester; mayoress; housewife.

Peter Butterworth

Peter Butterworth joined the Carry Ons as Doc in *Cowboy* in 1965. With his tubby figure, sensitive mobile face and jittery manner, he soon became an indispensable member of the team.

In real life he was a shy and gentle person and this was reflected in his Carry On roles, which were rarely bombastic but usually quietly and subtly potty. He was often cast as somebody else's stooge. As Detective-Constable Slobotham in *Screaming*, he is the fall-guy for his incompetent, thick-headed superior, Detective-Sergeant Bung (Harry H Corbett). As Citizen Bidet in *Don't Lose Your Head*, he has to stand by in helpless exasperation while his senior Secret Service officer, Citizen Camembert (Kenneth Williams), bungles all his chances. Peter's particular form of laid-back eccentricity comes into its own in *Camping*, as Joshua Fiddler, the shifty campsite manager who cons Sid James out of most of his cash. In *Behind*, his role as the scruffy and apparently furtive caravan-site handyman has a touching quality when Daphne (Joan Sims) claims him as her long-lost husband. He shines, too, as the elderly bootboy in *Emmannuelle*, whose teeth chatter uncontrollably as he recalls his most unusual sexual experience.

Perhaps the best of all his Carry On performances is his uncharacteristically flamboyant role in *Abroad*. As Pepe, the manager of an unfinished hotel who greets his unexpected guests in the guise of the builder, the porter, the receptionist and the telephone operator, he spends the first half of the film furiously trying to placate and accommodate them and the last half desperately trying to save the building from flood in a frenzied chaotic whirl.

Unlike most of the Carry On regulars, Peter Butterworth was a late starter in show business. Born in Bramhall, Cheshire in February, 1919, he was destined for a naval career, but in the Second World War he joined the Fleet Air Arm and was shot down by the Germans. In the prisoner-of-war camp he became very friendly with script-writer Talbot Rothwell, who persuaded him to take part in a camp concert, the aim of which was to drown out the noise of escaping prisoners. Peter, who had never performed in public before, was petrified, but he gamely sang a duet with Rothwell called 'The Letter Edged in Black', followed by some comic repartee which, according to his own account, provoked enough boos and hisses to have the desired effect. One of his dearest possessions was a photograph of the concert, which sparked off his determination to go into show business.

'Tolly' gave him every help and encouragement and after the war during a Jack Hylton summer show at Scarborough introduced him to the impressionist Janet Brown, whom he later married.

His face was well-known on TV in children's programmes and in shows with Ted Ray, Hugh Lloyd and Frankie Howerd. He also appeared on the stage in Whitehall farces, revues and pantomimes. Among his many film credits are *The Amorous Adventures of Moll Flanders* (1965), *Live Now, Pay Later* (1962), *The Day the Earth Caught Fire* (1961), *The Prince and the Pauper* (1962) and *A Funny Thing Happened on the Way to the Forum* (1966).

Above: one of Peter Butterworth's seediest characterizations is as Barnes, the campsite oddjobman in *Behind.*

Below: in *Dick*, Butterworth and his leader, Big Dick (Sid James), attempt to spring a surprise in the local jail right under the eyes of Captain Fancey (Kenneth Williams).

Above: Peter Butterworth's *pièce de resistance* of the Carry On films is his role in *Abroad* in which he plays Pepe, the harassed manager of an unfinished hotel in Spain whose property is not quite in one piece.

He died suddenly in January 1979, just before his 60th birthday, when he was due on the stage in Coventry to appear in pantomime. 'A thoroughly nice bloke and a dear friend', said Peter Rogers.

Carry On Years: 1965–1978 **Carry On Films:** 16

Carry On Titles: Cowboy; Screaming; Don't Lose Your Head; Follow That Camel; Doctor; Up The Khyber; Again Doctor; Camping; Loving; Henry; Abroad; Girls; Dick; Behind; England; Emmannuelle.

Carry On Professions: doctor; detective constable; secret policeman; valet; missionary; campsite manager; courtier; hotel manager; porter; switchboard operator; receptionist; naval officer; highwayman; verger; handyman; army officer; boot-boy.

Before Jack Douglas goes on holiday in **Carry On Behind** he gets locked up all night in the deep freeze of his butcher's shop. For his reappearance in the morning, apparently iced up and frozen stiff, he was coated all over in plastic and couldn't move a muscle. The team thought he had got off lightly, so they threw him into a bitterly cold lake to make up for his not having been actually frozen stiff.

Jack Douglas

With his gawky angular frame and jerky movements, Jack Douglas became a valuable acquisition for the later Carry Ons. He was born in Newcastle in 1927, to a theatrical family stretching back four generations. His grandfather was in silent films and his father was a Northern theatre impresario who put on variety shows and pantomimes all over England.

As a youngster during the war, Jack abandoned school for show business and worked for his father as a two-pounds-a-week dogsbody, doing everything from stage hand to carpenter and electrician. On three occasions his career has been helped by circumstances entirely beyond his control. The first was on his 15th birthday, when, the story goes, his father gave him a script for a pantomime and told him to go up to Sunderland to produce it. The second happened when the leading actor in one of the many pantomimes he had produced as a youngster fell ill. As nobody else knew the lines, Jack replaced him on stage. It gave him a taste for comedy acting and set him on his path.

His third accidental leap forward occurred when, after stooging for such topline comedians as Arthur Askey, Bruce Forsyth and Benny Hill, Jack teamed up with Joe Baker. When Baker somehow got locked out of a theatre, Jack had no option but to go on alone for the very first time. In nervous desperation, he began twitching and falling about – and the audience fell about, too. Thus was born his

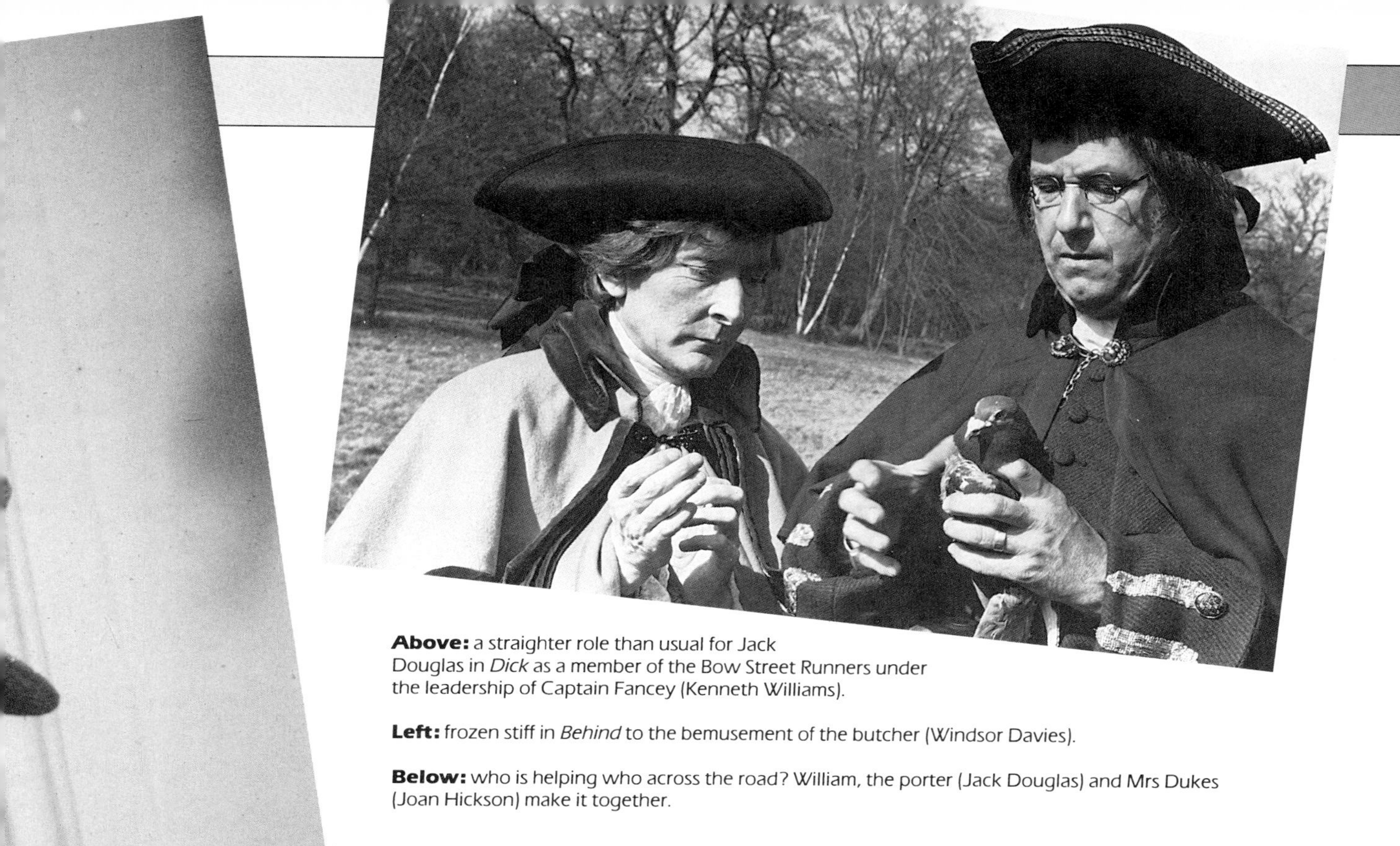

Above: a straighter role than usual for Jack Douglas in *Dick* as a member of the Bow Street Runners under the leadership of Captain Fancey (Kenneth Williams).

Left: frozen stiff in *Behind* to the bemusement of the butcher (Windsor Davies).

Below: who is helping who across the road? William, the porter (Jack Douglas) and Mrs Dukes (Joan Hickson) make it together.

comic stage character Alf Ippititimus who, in cloth cap and steel spectacles, became part of Jack's long-standing TV and stage partnership with Des O'Connor. Although he has now abandoned the Ippititimus image, it helped to shape his Carry On comic persona.

His first small roles in the series are pure Alf. The reeling and writhing hotel porter in *Girls*; and the fumbling, bumbling beer-drinker in *Abroad* who throws pints of beer over himself. But he came into his own in *Dick* as the nervy, clodhopping Sergeant Strapp, assigned to loo observation duty in the local tavern by Captain Fancey (Kenneth Williams) and slung out of the inn as a Peeping Tom. In *Behind* he is teamed up with Windsor Davies – two much-married men on the spree, trying to chat up a pair of bright young girls camping alongside their caravan and forgetting that they are no longer (if, indeed, they ever were) any young woman's dreamboys. Jack plays the naive slow-thinking Bragg who has to be nudged to understand that when Windsor Davies is talking about birds he doesn't mean ornithology.

In *England*, as Bombadier Ready, he supports the rebellious goings-on of Sergeants Willing and Able in his own gangling way. In *Emmannuelle* he has a key role as the butler Lyons (or Loins as Emmannuelle prefers to call him), leering and jerking his way through lecherous episodes and memories. His is a unique contribution to the series.

Douglas has a wide span of interests outside the world of comedy. He is a passionate jazz enthusiast with a huge collection of records, some of them rare. He paints a bit, designs his own clothes and is an expert on food and wine. He is an excellent cook and has had cookery books published, with Alf Ippititimus credited for some of the recipes.

Carry On Years: 1972–1978 **Carry On Films:** 7

Carry On Titles: Abroad; Matron; Girls; Dick; Behind; England; Emmannuelle.

Carry On Professions: hotel porter; Bow Street runner; butcher; soldier; butler.

Star Chart

	THE CARRY ON CORE									THE LOVELY LADIES										
	Kenneth Williams	Joan Sims	Charles Hawtrey	Sid James	Kenneth Connor	Hattie Jacques	Bernard Bresslaw	Terry Scott	Patsy Rowlands	Shirley Eaton	Liz Frazer	Barbara Windsor	Angela Douglas	Jacki Piper	Juliet Mills	Amanda Barrie	Dany Robin	Elke Sommer	Judy Geeson	Suzanne Danielle
Sergeant	*		*		*	*		*		*										
Nurse	*	*	*		*	*				*										
Teacher	*	*	*		*	*														
Constable	*	*	*	*	*	*				*										
Regardless	*	*	*	*	*	*					*									
Cruising	*			*	*						*									
Cabby			*	*	*	*					*					*				
Jack	*		*												*					
Spying	*		*									*								
Cleo	*	*	*	*	*											*				
Cowboy	*	*	*	*			*						*							
Screaming	*	*	*				*						*							
Don't Lose Your Head	*	*	*	*													*			
Follow That Camel	*	*	*				*						*							
Doctor	*	*	*	*		*	*					*								
Up The Khyber	*	*	*	*			*	*					*							
Again Doctor	*	*	*	*		*			*			*								
Camping	*	*	*	*		*	*	*				*								
Up The Jungle		*	*	*	*		*	*						*						
Loving	*	*	*	*		*	*	*	*					*						
Henry	*	*	*	*	*			*	*			*								
At Your Convenience	*	*	*	*		*	*		*					*						
Abroad	*	*	*	*	*	*	*		*			*								
Matron	*	*	*	*	*	*	*	*	*			*		*						
Girls		*		*	*		*		*			*								
Dick	*	*		*	*	*	*		*			*								
Behind	*	*			*		*		*		*							*		
England		*			*														*	
Emmannuelle	*	*			*															*

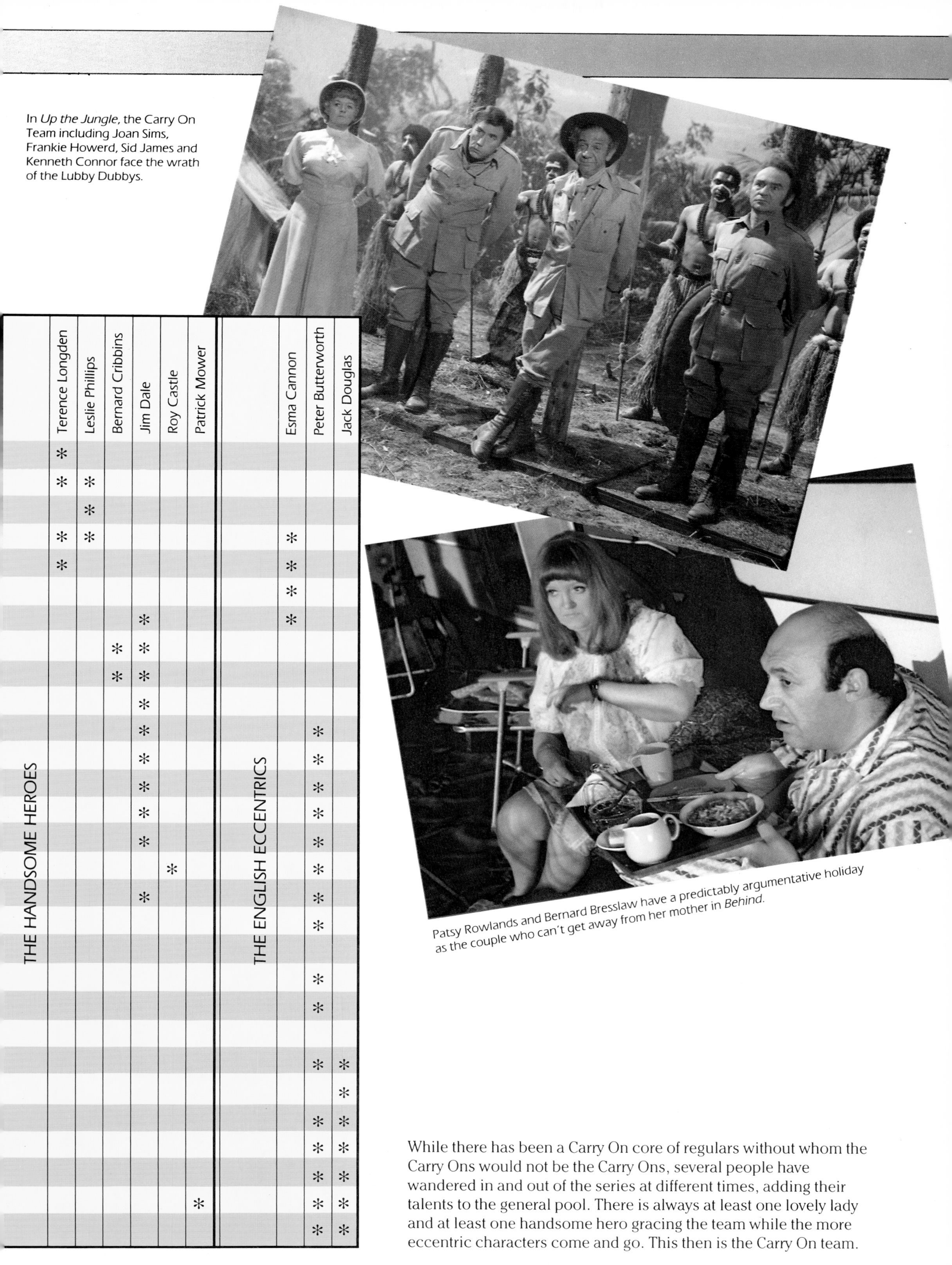

In *Up the Jungle*, the Carry On Team including Joan Sims, Frankie Howerd, Sid James and Kenneth Connor face the wrath of the Lubby Dubbys.

Patsy Rowlands and Bernard Bresslaw have a predictably argumentative holiday as the couple who can't get away from her mother in *Behind*.

THE HANDSOME HEROES	Terence Longden	Leslie Phillips	Bernard Cribbins	Jim Dale	Roy Castle	Patrick Mower	THE ENGLISH ECCENTRICS	Esma Cannon	Peter Butterworth	Jack Douglas
	*									
	*	*								
		*								
	*	*						*		
	*							*		
								*		
				*				*		
			*	*						
			*	*						
				*						
				*					*	
				*					*	
				*					*	
				*					*	
				*					*	
					*				*	
				*					*	
									*	
									*	
									*	
									*	*
										*
									*	*
									*	*
									*	*
						*			*	*
									*	*

While there has been a Carry On core of regulars without whom the Carry Ons would not be the Carry Ons, several people have wandered in and out of the series at different times, adding their talents to the general pool. There is always at least one lovely lady and at least one handsome hero gracing the team while the more eccentric characters come and go. This then is the Carry On team.

Carrying on Occasionally

Vincent Ball in *Follow That Camel.*

Appearing in smaller roles or one-off appearances in the Carry Ons is a galaxy of British comedy actors, supported by writers, singers, musicians, beauty queens, stand-up comics, a boxer and a parliamentary candidate. Some are obvious additions to the series, others more surprising.

TERENCE ALEXANDER, the popular actor best-known as Charlie Hungerford in TV's long-running series *Bergerac*, has a single scene in *Regardless* as the frustrated husband who can't understand a word that his German wife is shouting at him.

JOHN ANTROBUS, author of many bizarre comedies, including *The Bed-Sitting Room*, contributed some script additions to *Sergeant* and appears briefly in *Constable*, harassing the duty officer.

ROBIN ASKWITH, who plays the eager long-haired photographer Larry in *Girls*, is a well-known face from many TV series including *Please Sir* and *Dixon of Dock Green*. He appeared in most of the *Confession of a* . . . films and has written and directed several productions.

Robin Askwith plays Larry the photograpner who snaps the beauty queens in *Girls.*

NINA BADEN-SEMPER, one of the stars of TV's *Love Thy Neighbour*, is an uncredited member of the Nosher tribe in *Up The Jungle*.

SHAKIRA BAKSH, who plays Scrubba, one of Gladstone Screwer's many wives in *Again Doctor*, was Miss Guyana in the 1967 Miss World contest.

Publicity shot of Amanda Barrie as *Cleo.*

VINCENT BALL, the handsome Australian actor who appeared in many British films of the Fifties and Sixties including *A Town Like Alice* (1956), joined the team for two Carry Ons. In *Cruising*, he is the keep-fit instructor who makes all the girls go weak at the knees, while in *Follow That Camel* he is the ship's officer who checks Lady Ponsonby's porthole.

ERIC BARKER, actor and comedian who made his name starring with his wife Pearl Hackney in the radio programmes *Merry-Go-Round* and *Just Fancy*, was associated with a number of the early Carry Ons. He was the eccentric Captain Potts in *Sergeant*, the indecisive Inspector Mills in *Constable*, and the Chief in *Spying*. In addition, *Cruising* is based on one of his stories. He suffered a stroke which paralyzed him down one side and ended his Carry On career but, nevertheless, he returned for a small cameo, as the ancient General who enjoys the happenings under the dinner table in *Emmannuelle.*

AMANDA BARRIE started her Carry On career as a Glamcab driver in *Cabby* and graduated to the title role in *Cleo*. Born Shirley Ann Broadbent in Ashton-under-Lyme, she entered showbiz as one of Lionel Blair's dancers but first came to public attention as the hostess in the popular TV quiz show *Double Your Money*. In *Cabby*, she is one of the leggy lovelies whose ambition is to drive the men off the roads, but her Carry On highlight is undoubtedly her singleminded suburban Cleopatra who tempts Sid James' Mark Antony on to ever bigger and better things. In *Cleo*, there is an apt description of her as 'a siren of the Nile', whose 'hair is as black as ebony', whose 'face is like an ivory Goddess', and whose 'neck is like a swan'. Her comic rendering of the famous Egyptian Queen cocks a cheeky snook at Elizabeth Taylor in the more expensive version of this epic story. Barrie was most recently seen as the 'chip butty queen' Alma Sedgwick in *Coronation Street* in the early Eighties.

WILFRED BRAMBELL, famous as Steptoe Senior, plays another 'dirty old man' in *Again Doctor* – a long-suffering patient who needs regular hormone injections. He died in 1985.

PETER BYRNE, well-remembered as Detective Crawford, the son-in-law of TV's *Dixon of Dock Green*, has a small role as a bridegroom in *Cabby*.

ESMA CANNON, the diminutive character actress, adds her unique style of twittering comedy to the Carry On series in several roles. Born in Australia, she came to Britain in the early Thirties and played numerous big and little screen roles, usually cast as a maiden aunt or a busybody. She found a wider audience when she appeared in *The Rag Trade*, but she found her comic niche when she joined the Carry On team. In *Constable*, she plays a deaf old lady who is furious with Kenneth Williams for 'helping' her across a road which she has just succeeded in negotiating by herself the other way. In *Regardless*, she is Sid's assistant, administrating the Helping Hands agency and throwing it into confusion with her new filing system. As Flo in *Cabby*, she is a doddery battleaxe, determined to drive her husband's cab in spite of a threat to strike if a woman takes the wheel. And she excels as the high-spirited passenger who reminds the Captain of a 'mad little pixie' in *Cruising*.

Wilfred Brambell takes liberties with a passing nurse in *Again Doctor*.

In *Cruising*, Esma Cannon samples all the delights of the local resorts.

Roy Castle in *Up The Khyber*.

JOHNNY BRIGGS, better-known as *Coronation Street*'s Mike Baldwin, appears as one of the kilted Third Foot and Mouth Regiment in *Up The Khyber*, as a plasterer in *Behind*, and as the Major's put-upon driver in *England*.

RAY BROOKS, who made his name in the Sixties in films like *The Knack* (1965) and *Cathy Come Home* (1966), plays Georgio, the bartender who broadens Evelyn Blunt's horizons in *Abroad*. He is now well-known as the star of the TV series *Big Deal* and *Running Wild*.

DORA BRYAN, the popular comedienne, star of many revues and stage shows including *Gentlemen Prefer Blondes* and *Hello, Dolly*, has a lively role as the NAAFI girl who falls for the weakling Horace Strong in *Sergeant*. She won a British Academy Award for her performance in *A Taste of Honey* (1961).

PATRICK CARGILL, known to TV viewers as the harassed parent in *Father, Dear Father*, has been associated with three Carry Ons. In collaboration with Jack Searle he created the idea on which *Nurse* is based; he has a small cameo as Dom Luise, the smooth Spanish governor threatened by the crew of the 'Venus' in *Jack*; and he has a small part in *Regardless*.

ROY CASTLE, the popular cabaret artiste, plays the romantic lead in *Up The Khyber* as the very British Captain Keene, falling in love with Princess Jehli and saving the garrison from destruction. He plays the part almost straight, emphasizing the madness around him, particularly in the famous dinner scene where he is finally moved to ask if he might 'have a bash' at the enemy himself. Castle started in entertainment as a stooge for Jimmy James but his many talents, which include dancing and playing the trumpet, soon made him an international cabaret star. His stage hits include the Broadway production of *Pickwick*, with Harry Secombe, and the revival of *Singin' in the Rain*, with Tommy Steele. He is a TV personality who hosts his own shows including *Record Breakers*.

CYRIL CHAMBERLAIN was one of those indispensable supporting players in British cinema, usually cast in solid, dependable roles. He appears, true to type, in the first seven Carry Ons, displaying light touch.

JEREMY CONNOR made his first appearance in *Nurse* at the tender age of 3½. The son of Kenneth, he can be seen as a footpad in *Dick*, a student in *Behind* and a gunner in *England*.

Left: Cyril Carter (Kenneth Cope) is having problems.

Bernard Cribbins plays secret agent Harold Crump, surveying the Casbah, in *Spying*.

In *Screaming* Harry H Corbett comes face to face with Oddbod and Oddbod junior.

PAT COOMBS, the well-loved TV personality and comedienne and star of numerous TV sit-coms including *You Only Live Twice*, is a rebellious patient in *Doctor* and the new snooty matron in *Again Doctor*.

KENNETH COPE made his first foray into Carry On territory as Cyril, the petty thief in *Matron*, who infiltrates the hospital in nurse's guise and is so convincing he gets roped in for ambulance duty. He followed up with the less sympathetic role of the obtuse shop steward in *At Your Convenience*. He has had a wide-ranging career, tasting nationwide fame as Sonny Jim in *Coronation Street* and, in contrast, playing comedy satire in *That Was the Week That Was*. He later gained popularity as the ghostly Hopkirk in *Randall and Hopkirk (Deceased)* and he has written scripts for TV.

HARRY H CORBETT, who played Harold in TV's *Steptoe and Son* for 13 years, joined the Carry On team as the useless Detective-Inspector Bung in *Screaming*. Despite his Sherlock Holmes cape and deerstalker, there is nothing canny about Bung – he is quite capable of missing all the clues, particularly when there is a pretty woman around. Perhaps his best line in the film (and he has many good ones), occurs when his assistant points out a remarkable similarity in the files relating to the cases of disappearing women they are examining. 'That's not so surprising', Bung replies 'we buy all our files at the same shop'. Corbett was awarded the OBE in 1976. He died in 1982.

HOWARD MARION CRAWFORD, the beefy character actor whose radio work earned him the epitaph 'the man with the 1,000 voices' has a small cameo as a wine-taster in *Regardless*. He died in 1969.

BERNARD CRIBBINS joined the early Carry Ons with two major roles. He took the lead in *Jack*, as the gentlemanly greenhorn Midshipman Poop-Decker who is robbed of his clothes, captured by the press-gang and consigned to menial duties below decks. Against all odds, he becomes the hero of the British navy. In *Spying*, he plays Harold Crump, one of the bungling trainee secret agents who can destroy even the best-laid plans. He does, however, get the girl. A light comedy actor and a recording artiste who specializes in nonsense songs, Cribbins has starred in many films including the children's feature *The Railway Children* (1970) and *The Water Babies* (1978).

SUZANNE DANIELLE, the sex symbol who was known as The Body after her performance in *The Stud* (1978), plays the title role in *Emmannuelle*. She is a lady of many talents who has, amongst other things, played a robot in *Dr Who*, been a hostess on TV's *3-2-1* and impersonated Lady Di opposite Mike Yarwood's Prince Charles. She is now a TV personality and a regular panellist on game shows like *Blankety-Blank*.

WINDSOR DAVIES, the Cockney-born Welshman, pops up in two of the later Carry Ons. In *Behind*, he plays Fred Ramsden, a much-married man trying – and failing miserably – to indulge in a middle-aged spree at a holiday caravan site. In *England*, he has a more familiar role as the ranting Sergeant Major 'Tiger' Bloomer – a variation of his popular TV role in *It Ain't Half Hot, Mum*. The son of a miner, Davies worked in the pits before becoming an actor. He started his career in classical roles but found his forte in comedy. He teamed up with Don Estelle, the little trouper he bullies mercilessly throughout *It Ain't Half Hot, Mum*, toured with him as a double act, and had a big chart success with their comic recording of 'Whispering Grass'. More recently, he has starred as one of the warring antique dealer neighbours in *Never the Twain*.

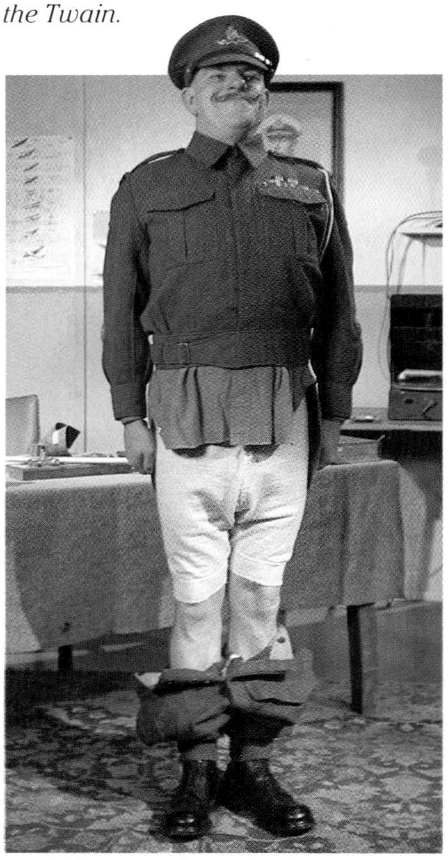

Sergeant-Major Bloomer (Windsor Davies), caught out again, in *England*.

JERRY DESMONDE, who appears in *Regardless* as an actor looking for someone to rehearse with, was a well-known music-hall artiste, best remembered as a peerless straight man for Sid Field and later Norman Wisdom. He died in 1967.

ANGELA DOUGLAS took on the female glamour role in four historical Carry Ons, bridging the gap between Liz Fraser and Barbara Windsor. Her debut, in *Cowboy*, as the fast-shooting Annie Oakley out to avenge her father's death, sets the style for her characters. In the series, she usually plays a seemingly innocent English rose whose shy exterior hides a passionate and gutsy woman. In *Screaming*, she suffers the indignity of vitrification and is turned into a shop dummy. In *Follow That Camel*, she plays Lady Jane Ponsonby who travels half way round the world to find her lover, coyly tasting all the delights of the journey. And in *Up The Khyber*, her last Carry On, she is Princess Jelhi, the daughter and 'light of my darkness' of the Khazi of Kalabar. In her first three Carry Ons, she is teamed with Jim Dale, with whom she later appeared in *Digby, the Biggest Dog in the World* (1973). Douglas was a teenage actress in repertory who went on to play in numerous stage shows and films. She married Kenneth More and cut back her acting commitments for a while to concentrate on home life. After More's death, she returned to work, adding writing to her talents, publishing her autobiography and contributing to newspapers and magazines. She can still be seen on TV shows like *Give Us a Clue*.

SHIRLEY EATON, the famous golden girl of the James Bond movie *Goldfinger* (1964), provides the love interest in the early Carry Ons. In *Sergeant*, she plays Mary, the bride deserted on her wedding night when her husband is called up. She follows him to camp and finally gets her man. In *Nurse*, she plays Dorothy, the nurse who falls in love with her patient. When he is discharged, she finally gets her man. In *Constable*, she has jitters before the wedding but, after some counselling from Constable Potter, she gets her man. Eaton was a child actress who later had an act at the London Palladium with Max Bygraves. The highlight of her screen career was as the Bond girl who is suffocated by being painted from head to toe in gold paint. She abandoned acting in 1968 to concentrate on her family.

E V H EMMETT, the celebrated commentator who worked for Gaumont-British News and then for Universal News during the Thirties and Forties, gave *Cleo's* satirical commentary an authentic ring.

DAVID ESSEX, the actor and pop singer, had a small part in *Henry*, only his scene hit the cutting-room floor and he does not appear in the final film.

Bert Handy (Sid James) sizes up a potential worker (Liz Fraser) in *Regardless*.

FENELLA FIELDING, with her dark, smouldering beauty and purring seductive voice, is as much at home in strong dramatic roles as she is in comedy. She has played the title role in *Hedda Gabler* and Nora in *The Doll's House*, and was in the TV production of *The Importance of Being Earnest*. But in films she is known as a humorous vamp, and the Carry Ons put her talents to good use. As Penny Panting in *Regardless*, she applies to the Helping Hands agency for a male baby-sitter but she really wants a man – to make her husband jealous. In *Screaming*, the second of her two Carry Ons, she excels as the mysterious and sinister Valeria who, together with her brother, the 'undead' Dr Watt, is up to no good in the cellars of their crumbling old mansion.

LIZ FRASER was born Elizabeth Winch in 1933. Her first venture into showbiz was in Tony Hancock's TV series but she made her name playing dumb blondes in films like *I'm All Right, Jack* (1959) and *Up the Junction* (1967). She specializes in light comedy and, for a while, she took the romantic lead in the Carry Ons. She was in three of the early entries: in *Cabby*, she plays Kenneth Connor's girlfriend, the spy in the male camp; in *Cruising*, she is Gladys Trimble, a shapely passenger with an eye for the men; in *Regardless*, she is one of the Helping Hands, as eager for excitement and adventure as any of the men. Her Carry On personality was that of the down-to-earth girl-next-door, sexy but not too naughty. She returned to the Carry Ons to play Sylvia in *Behind*. At around the same period she had a number of parts in the *Confessions of a . . .* films and is now a TV personality and veteran of game shows like *Give Us a Clue*.

Fenella Fielding plays the seductive vamp Valeria, the queen of horror, in *Screaming*.

JUDITH FURSE was a large actress who specialized in ruthless roles. She brought her expertise to three Carry Ons. In *Regardless*, she has a cameo as a dragon of a teacher in charge of a party of schoolchildren. In *Cabby*, she is a battleaxe, but her main Carry On role was in *Spying* as Dr Crow, the evil head of STENCH, the Society for the Extermination of Non-Conforming Humans. She died in 1974.

JUDY GEESON, who started her career as a sexy teenager in films like *To Sir, With Love* (1967) and *Here We Go Round the Mulberry Bush* (also 1967) stars as Sergeant Tilly Willing opposite Patrick Mower's Ken Able in *England.*

SALLY GEESON, Judy's younger sister, is best-known as Sid James' daughter in *Bless This House*. She plays young, leggy girls in two Carry Ons – Lily in *Abroad* and Debra in *Girls*.

PETER GILMORE started his Carry On life as a petty gangster in *Cabby*; rose to the rank of galley master in *Cleo*; is glimpsed as the gentleman cad who shoots himself at the beginning of *Follow That Camel*; becomes the exalted Citizen Robespierre in *Don't Lose Your Head*; and changes sides to ascend the throne of France in *Henry*. As the King of France, one of his larger Carry On roles, his foppish manners and velvet-gloved finery mask a mailed-fist determination to make war on England if Henry fails to restore conjugal rights to his cousin, Marie of Normandy. Gilmore has appeared in nine Carry Ons. He is a singer as well as an actor, and one of his favourite roles was that of MacHeath in *The Beggars' Opera*. He gained national fame in the TV series *A Man Called Intrepid* and as the star of *The Onedin Line*.

DERYCK GUYLER, who first made his name in the radio programme ITMA and later delighted audiences as the grumpy caretaker in the long-running TV comedy series *Please, Sir,* plays a doddery surgeon in *Doctor*.

SHEILA HANCOCK, the brilliant comedy actress who became a stage director at the Cambridge Arts Theatre and the Royal Shakespeare Company, gives a remarkable cameo performance as Senna, the nagging wife of Hengist Pod, in *Cleo*.

IRENE HANDL, the veteran comedy actress and best-selling novelist, appeared in two Carry Ons. In *Nurse*, she plays in one of director Gerald Thomas' favourite vignettes as the wife who bores her husband to tears with talk of insurance forms. In *Constable*, she turns up as an irate mum in search of her little Willie. Although she died in 1987, she can still be seen on TV whenever *For the Love of Ada* is repeated.

ANITA HARRIS, the Sixties singing star, is Corktip in *Follow That Camel*, a belly dancer, fortune teller and temptress who is an agent for the Sheik, and Nurse Clark in *Doctor*, one of Dr Kilmore's many fans.

WILLIAM HARTNELL, who featured in scores of British films and had the distinction of being the first Dr Who, is Sergeant Grimshawe in *Sergeant*, the NCO with the unenviable job of knocking the motley bunch of recruits into shape. He died in 1975.

IMOGEN HASSALL, the actress who was once known as The Countess of Cleavage, plays Jenny Grub in *Loving*, the shy and protected young girl who comes out in a big way with the help of the Wedded Bliss Agency. Later, she tried to loose her busty image, joining the Royal Shakespeare Company. She died in 1980.

Left: Bagshaw (Peter Gilmore) expires of shame in *Follow That Camel* attended by the doctor (Julian Orchard), Lady Ponsonby (Angela Douglas) and her father (William Mervyn).

Below: Irene Handl bores her husband (Bill Owen) to distraction in *Nurse*.

Above: Patricia Hayes plays Mrs Beasley, a patient with a lengthy list of complaints for Dr Nookey (Jim Dale) in *Again Doctor*.

Above left: Corktip, the dancer, played by Anita Harris, is surrounded by problems in *Follow That Camel*.

CAROL HAWKINS, who plays the luscious Sharon in *Please, Sir*, appears in two Carry Ons. In *Abroad*, she plays Marge, a holidaymaker looking for some action. In *Behind*, she tries to escape the amorous attentions of two married men.

MELVYN HAYES shot to fame in Cliff Richard's *The Young Ones* (1961), and is now known from *It Ain't Half Hot, Mum* and other comedy series. He features in *England* as Gunner Shorthouse.

PATRICIA HAYES, veteran of countless comedies including *Till Death Us Do Part* and *The Lady is a Tramp* and highly acclaimed for her TV performance in *Edna, the Inebriate Woman*, plays Mrs Beasley, a talkative patient, in *Again Doctor*.

PERCY HERBERT, a character actor familiar as a Cockney soldier in films like *The Bridge on The River Kwai* (1957), *Tunes of Glory* (1960) and *The Guns of Navarone* (1961), plays two 'tough guys' in the Carry Ons – Mr Angel, the disciplinarian bosun in *Jack*, and Charlie, the hard-talking barman in *Cowboy*.

DONALD HEWLETT, best known as one of the incompetent officers in *It Ain't Half Hot, Mum*, plays the Dean who despatches the unlikely pair of archaeologists on a dig in *Behind*.

JOAN HICKSON. After many TV, screen and stage roles, usually as an understanding mother or an eccentric aunt, Joan Hickson shot to fame as Agatha Christie's Miss Marple. She is the officious sister in *Nurse*, an aristocratic drunk in *Constable*, a matron in *Regardless*, Jenny Grub's over-protective mother in *Loving*, and the old girl who needs help to cross the road in *Girls*.

JULIAN HOLLOWAY, son of the famous comedian and character actor Stanley Holloway, is a Carry On stalwart with seven supporting roles to his credit. He is the ticket collector – one of Lady Ponsonby's many seducers – in *Follow That Camel*; the coach driver who accidentally tears off Barbara Windsor's nightie in *Camping*; and the long-suffering Major who assists Sir Sidney Ruff-Diamond in *Up The Khyber*.

LINDA HOOKS, a beauty queen and hostess of TV's *Sale of the Century*, makes several appearances in Carry Ons. She is one of Madame Desirée's Birds of Paradise in *Dick* and plays nurses in both *Behind* and *England*.

DONALD HOUSTON, the Welsh actor with over 300 movies to his credit, including many adventure films like *Where Eagles Dare* (1968) and *The Sea Wolves* (1980), plays the vicious First Lieutenant in *Jack*.

RENEE HOUSTON, the outstanding Scottish character actress who toured the music halls between the wars as half of the celebrated Houston Sisters act, appears in small roles in *Cabby* and *Spying* and gives a powerful performance as Kenneth Cope's domineering mum in *At Your Convenience*.

FRANKIE HOWERD, the famous stand-up comic with his unique oohs and aahs, appeared in two Carry Ons. in *Doctor*, he plays Frances Bigger, the mind-over-matter evangelist who bolts for the safety of hospital at the first sign of illness. In *Up The Jungle*, he gives a memorable performance as Professor Inigo Tinkle, the pompous ornithologist on the look-out for the legendary oozalum bird. Howerd, who once said that he thought the Carry Ons meant more to the general public than Shakespeare, has his own distinctive persona which meshes in perfectly with the Carry On style. Considered by many to be Britain's top comic artist, Howerd made his name in revues in the Fifties. His lead in the stage version of *A Funny Thing Happened on the Way to the Forum* brought him to the attention of TV and he had a new lease of life on the small screen in shows like *The Frankie Howerd Show* and *Up Pompeii* (the latter written by Carry On's Talbot Rothwell). He was awarded the OBE in 1977 for his works for charity and in 1983, he suffered an accident which severely limited his ability to carry on.

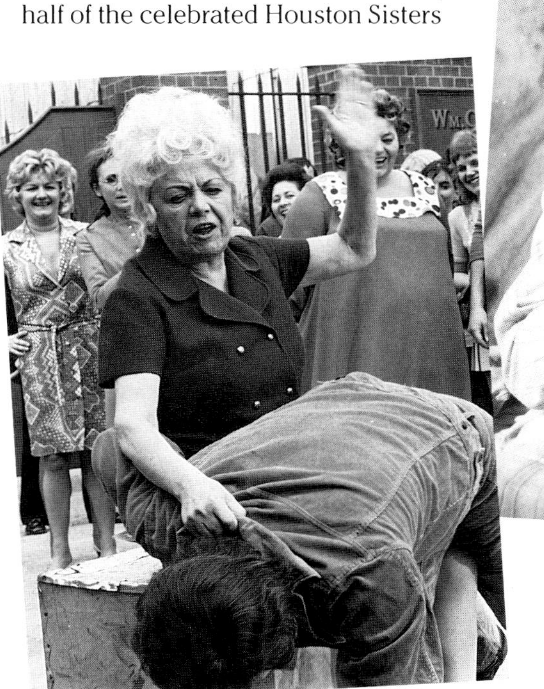

Left: Mrs Spanner (Renee Houston) knocks some sense into her son (Kenneth Cope) in *At Your Convenience*.

Above: in *Up The Jungle*, Professor Inigo Tinkle (Frankie Howerd) is prepared for anything to happen at night.

Geoffrey Hughes in *At Your Convenience.*

GEOFFREY HUGHES, better known as Eddie Yates in *Coronation Street*, can be seen among the striking workers in *At Your Convenience*.

WILFRID HYDE-WHITE, who played numerous government officials in films and TV, made a memorable guest star appearance in *Nurse* as the Colonel, a 'naughty old buzzer' who drives the nurses wild with his betting but gets his comeuppance with a daffodil. His agent threatened to sue, claiming that somebody else's bottom was used for the gag. He withdrew when it was pointed out that no bottom actually appears in the sequence – it is all done by suggestion. The last laugh came when Hyde-White gamely admitted that he hadn't read the script before agreeing to the role – he had simply jumped at the chance of a free ticket home from Hollywood in time for the Grand National.

JILL IRELAND who starred opposite her husband Charles Bronson in *Death Wish II* (1982) and many other films, makes a brief appearance in *Nurse*, falling in love with snooty Kenneth Williams when she visits him in hospital.

PETER JONES, the actor and playwright who is perhaps best-known on TV as the harassed boss of *The Rag Trade* and, more recently, in *Beggar My Neighbour*, appears in two Carry Ons. He is the chaplain in *Doctor* and the wisecracking Brigadier in *England*, getting one of the best lines. 'Whose flag is that?' he asks as a pair of bloomers are hoisted up the flagpole, 'Knicaragua?'

PENELOPE KEITH, the snobbish neighbour from *The Good Life* and the star of *To the Manor Born*, makes a brief appearance as a gawky nurse in *Doctor*.

BILL KENWRIGHT, producer of many West End shows and featured in *Coronation Street* as Gordon Clegg, plays a reporter in *Matron*.

DAVID KERNAN, who starred in the hit show *Side by Side by Sondheim*, plays Nicholas in *Abroad*.

ROSALIND KNIGHT, a busy stage and screen actress, plays two interesting roles in the early Carry Ons. In *Nurse*, she makes a brief but memorable impact as the plain, awkward Nurse Nightingale whose dull job is to monitor a patient's drip feed. In *Teacher*, she had a larger part as Felicity Wheeler, the woman from the Ministry who is investigating the school but falls for Kenneth Connor's bumbling charms.

IAN LAVENDER, the 'mother's boy' Private Pike of *Dad's Army*, turns up on the caravan site in *Behind* as Joe Baxter.

DILYS LAYE is a variety actress who played in several Carry Ons. In *Spying*, she is a nightclub singer, a beautiful temptress who turns out to be a double agent. Thereafter she is something of a weakling who reveals her tough core in the end. In *Cruising*, she is shyly on the look out for a husband. She comes into her own in *Camping* as the nervous Anthea who is sick at the slightest provocation but who eventually finds true happiness with Bernard Bresslaw. She also appeared in *Doctor*. Outside of the Carry Ons, she is best-known for her roles in *The Bed-Sit Girl* with Sheila Hancock and in *The Boy Friend* on Broadway with Julie Andrews. She wrote the Granada TV series *Chintz*.

GEORGE LAYTON, who makes a brief appearance in *Behind* as a doctor, is very versatile. A TV personality and quizmaster, he has scripted several TV series including *Robin's Nest* and *Don't Wait Up*. He has been a presenter on *That's Life* and was one of the interns in TV's *Doctor in the House.*

HENRY LIVINGS is an actor and playwright and the author of off-beat plays with titles like *Big Soft Nellie*, *Stop It, Whoever You Are*, and *Eh?*. He has a tiny part as one of the recruits in *Sergeant*.

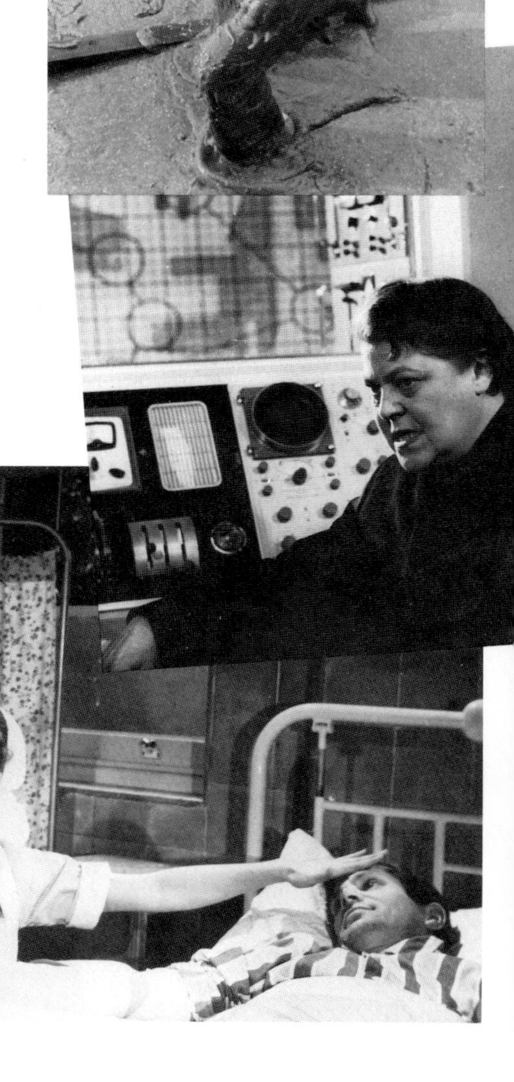

JIMMY LOGAN, the Scottish comedian, makes two appearances in the Carry Ons. In *Abroad*, he pips Sid James to the post and walks away with Barbara Windsor – but only after he has twice fallen face-first into wet concrete. In *Girls*, he makes an uncharacteristic appearance as the camp TV presenter who joins in the melée around the beauty competition.

TERENCE LONGDEN was a regular part of the early Carry On team, appearing in four of the first five films. His upper-class veneer adds a different comic element to the series. In *Sergeant*, he is Miles Heywood, a recruit pronounced 'a soldier by tradition and by instinct' when he admits that the first thing that comes into his head is always women. In *Nurse*, he is the journalist with appendicitis who supplies the romantic interest in the story. In *Constable*, he is a smooth conman, and in *Regardless*, he is the most debonair of the Helping Hands. As an actor, Longden can turn his hand to a variety of parts. He trained at RADA and has been a classical actor at Stratford. He was Drusus in the 1959 version of *Ben Hur* and popped up as one of Elsie Tanner's followers in *Coronation Street*. He had the title role in the TV series *Garry Haliday*.

Left: Bert (Jimmy Logan) finds unfinished hotels can be very sticky in *Abroad*.

Lila (Dilys Laye) turns the tables on Dr Crow (Judith Furse) in *Spying*.

Michael Medwin makes a guest appearance in *Nurse* as boxing promoter Ginger visiting one of his boys

KENNY LYNCH, the popular entertainer, contributes a good one-liner to the Carry Ons as the bus conductor in *Loving*, asking the fully-occupied courting couple if they are 'going all the way?'. He also wrote 'Love Crazy', the title song of *Emmannuelle*.

Left: Rosalind Knight plays the eagle-eyed Nurse Nightingale, on bedside duty in *Nurse*.

In *At Your Convenience*, Bill Maynard plays the commercial traveller who likes a regular life.

ELSPETH MARCH, veteran character actress specializing in imposing upper-class roles – she was the Dowager Empress in *Anastasia* (1967) – appears in *Again Doctor* as a member of the hospital board and gives a superb uncredited cameo as an English aristocrat in *Don't Lose Your Head*.

BETTY MARSDEN, who made her name with her many roles in radio's *Round the Horn*, is in two Carry Ons. She has a small part in *Regardless* as the siren on the train who convinces Kenneth Connor he is mixed up in a spy adventure. But she really makes her mark on the series in *Camping*, playing Harriet Potter with an unforgettable screeching laugh which drives her long-suffering husband round the bend.

BILL MAYNARD is in six of the later Carry Ons. His parts are usually small cameos and there is one uncredited performance (in *Abroad*). In *Henry*, he is Guy Fawkes, continually popping up with his gunpowder at the ready; in *At Your Convenience*, he is Joan Sims' husband, obsessed with an orderly life; in *Matron*, he is one of Sid's gang, and he also turns up in *Loving* and *Dick*. He is the star of the TV series *Oh No, It's Selwyn Froggitt* and he stood against Tony Benn as an independent candidate in the Chesterfield by-election.

MICHAEL MEDWIN, the sandy-haired actor and producer whose career stretches from *The Army Game* to *Shoestring*, made a brief guest appearance in *Nurse* as Kenneth Connor's boxing promoter.

FREDDIE MILLS, the former world light heavyweight boxing champion, turns up as a crook in *Constable* and, closer to home, as a fight arranger in need of seconds in *Regardless*. He met a violent death in the mid-Sixties.

JULIET MILLS, the daughter of Sir John Mills and the sister of Hayley, cast away her goody-goody image from the US TV series *The Nanny and the Professor* to star as Sally, the barmaid who impersonates a midshipman in *Jack*. Playing the romantic lead opposite Bernard Cribbins (the sailor whose place she takes), Mills is nevertheless more prim than most of the Carry On Ladies.

WARREN MITCHELL, who became immortalised as Alf Garnett in *Till Death Us Do Part* and its successor, plays the streetwise Ancient Roman slave-auctioneer Spencius (the brother of Marcus) in *Cleo*.

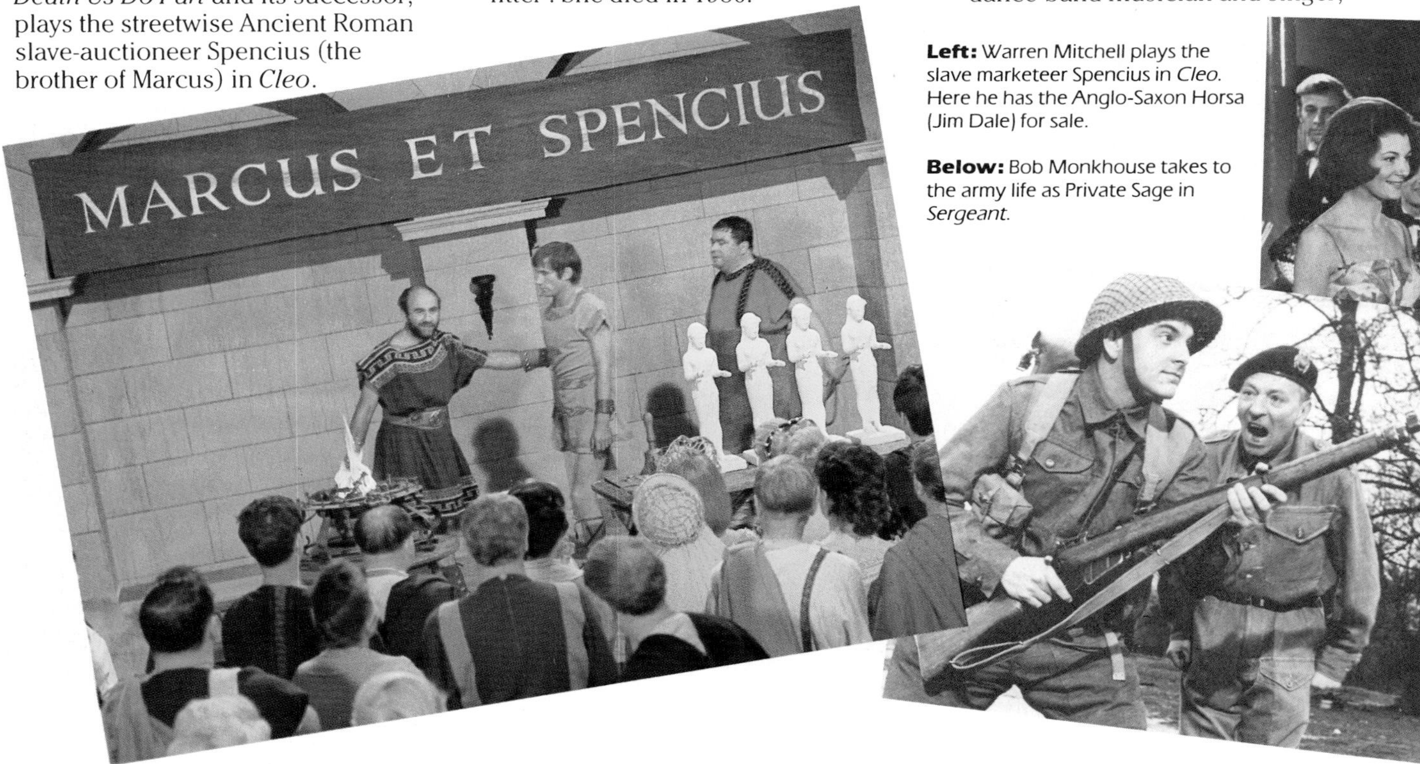

Left: Warren Mitchell plays the slave marketeer Spencius in *Cleo*. Here he has the Anglo-Saxon Horsa (Jim Dale) for sale.

Below: Bob Monkhouse takes to the army life as Private Sage in *Sergeant*.

BOB MONKHOUSE was in the first Carry On. In *Sergeant*, a very youthful Monkhouse plays Charlie, the groom who is called up on his wedding night. His romantic charm was an asset, but he did not stay with the team. Monkhouse, who trained as an animator, worked as a joke writer for people like Bob Hope and is a 'movie buff' with a large collection of old films. He is the host of numerous TV quiz shows including *The Golden Shot*, *Celebrity Squares*, *Family Fortunes*, *Bob's Full House* and *Bob Says Opportunity Knocks*. His talent for fast and humorous ad-libbing makes them all entertaining family shows.

PATRICK MOWER, the good-looking actor who made his name playing tough cops in programmes like *Callan*, *Special Branch* and *Target*, makes a rare excursion into comedy with *England*. He plays Sergeant Able, the leader of the men's barrack room in the experimental mixed camp.

DANDY NICHOLS, the veteran character actress much-loved as Alf Garnett's long-suffering wife in *Till Death Us Do Part*, plays Sid James' wife in *Doctor* and contributes a classic Carry On one-liner when he asks, 'Is it my fault that the labour couldn't find me a job?' 'Yes', she replies deadpan, 'when you put yourself down as a hansom cab lamp fitter'. She died in 1986.

RICHARD O'CALLAGHAN, the son of comedienne Patricia Hayes, is now a serious stage actor, but he started his career playing two young lads in the Carry Ons. In *Loving*, he is the innocent Bertie Muffet who registers his hobbies at the Wedded Bliss agency as making model airplanes out of milk bottle tops. In *At Your Convenience*, he plays the snobbish Lewis Boggs, the son of the factory owner, whose new-fangled ideas bring him into conflict with the unions.

MILO O'SHEA, the Irish character actor associated with the Abbey Theatre in Dublin, can be seen amongst Sid James' taxi drivers in *Cabby*.

RICHARD O'SULLIVAN, the TV sit-com actor and star of *Man About the House*, *Robin's Nest* and *Me and My Girl*, is Robin Stevens, the leader of the young saboteurs in *Teacher*. The mastermind behind the campaign to keep the headmaster at the school, O'Sullivan displays all the comedy potential he later developed on TV.

BILL OWEN is in three of the early Carry Ons. In *Sergeant*, he plays Corporal Copping, battling against all odds to kick some sense into the new recruits. In *Nurse*, he is an impatient patient with his leg slung up in plaster. And in *Cabby* he plays Smiley, one of Sid's drivers. Owen, who has been a dance-band musician and singer, made his feature film debut in *The Way to the Stars* (1945) and is known to millions as Compo, the scruffy senile delinquent in the TV comedy series *Last of the Summer Wine*.

CECIL PARKER, a well-known character actor and revue artist, and flustered upper-class gent of many a British film, is on good form as the First Sea Lord of the Admiralty in *Jack*. He died in 1971.

NICHOLAS PARSONS. Known to millions of TV viewers as the host of *Sale of the Century*, he has a small role as the lecherous wine-taster in *Regardless*.

LANCE PERCIVAL, the comedian with the lopsided toothy grin, appears in *Cruising* as Haines, the ship's chef, who has some bizarre ideas about cooking. He landed the part when one of the Carry On regulars opted out and he fitted into the Carry On style immediately. Percival, who entered showbusiness with a calypso group, was spotted by Peter Rogers in *One Over the Eight*, a stage revue starring Sheila Hancock. About the same time, he was also spotted by Ned Sherrin, who promptly signed him up for the TV satire *That Was The Week That Was*, for which he wrote and performed skits and songs. An accident in 1970 took him out of the business for a while but he returned as a writer (he scripted *Whodunnit* for Thames Television), an inventor of game shows and a TV guest on programmes like Channel 4's word game show *Countdown*, where he appeared in Dictionary Corner.

Above: Ship's chef Wilfred Haines (Lance Percival) presents a cake of his own concoction for the Captain's table in *Cruising*.

BILL PERTWEE, the ARP warden of *Dad's Army*, was a barman in *Loving* and the fire brigade chief who debags the mayor in *Girls*. He is a veteran of *Round the Horn* and second cousin to the other showbusiness Pertwees – Jon and Michael.

JON PERTWEE, who made his name as *Dr Who*, gives three delightful Carry On cameo performances. In *Cleo*, he is a soothsayer, conjuring up visions of disaster; in *Cowboy*, he is the decrepit Sheriff Albert Earp, brought to a sudden end by the Rumpo Kid; and in *Screaming* he plays Dr Fettle, the police surgeon destroyed, Frankenstein-like, by his own creation.

LESLIE PHILLIPS is always thought of as a central member of the Carry On team although he appears only three times. In *Nurse*, he is a jovial cad, sipping champagne while waiting for an operation on his bunion. In *Teacher*, he is a 'noxious ninny' of a child psychiatrist, trying to test out his trendy theories. And in *Constable*, he is a rookie who turns up for duty with a tennis racquet under his arm. When he left the series, the part of the upper-class bounder was dropped. A former child actor, Phillips is an accomplished light comedian who made his name in the Carry On and Doctor films. He also starred in radio's *The Navy Lark*, which ran for 14 years. He specializes in playing those who are not bred for hard graft. More recently, he has appeared in stage farces like *The Man Most Likely To . . .*

Above: Constable Porter (Leslie Phillips) blunders his way through the back gardens of Thurston in *Constable*.

JACKI PIPER is the romantic interest in three Carry Ons. As Sally, in *Loving*, she is a model who falls for shy Bertie Muffet after several comic misunderstandings. In *Up The Jungle*, she is June to Terry Scott's overgrown Jungle Boy. And in *At Your Convenience* she plays the canteen worker who inspires both the boss' son and the union leader. She is also the Sister in *Matron*. Her ability to melt into the background earns the admiration of Mr Boozy in *Up The Jungle*, where she is dressed to her neck as a Victorian maid. He tells her, 'you could walk starkers through a Foreign Legion outpost and nothing would happen'. With only a slight change of style, she can become a luscious beauty, a talent which made her a valuable part of the team.

Above: Dandy Nichols plays a humorous cameo as Sid James's nagging wife in *Doctor*.
Below: Sally (Jacki Piper) and Bertie (Richard O'Callaghan) have got their wires crossed in *Loving*.

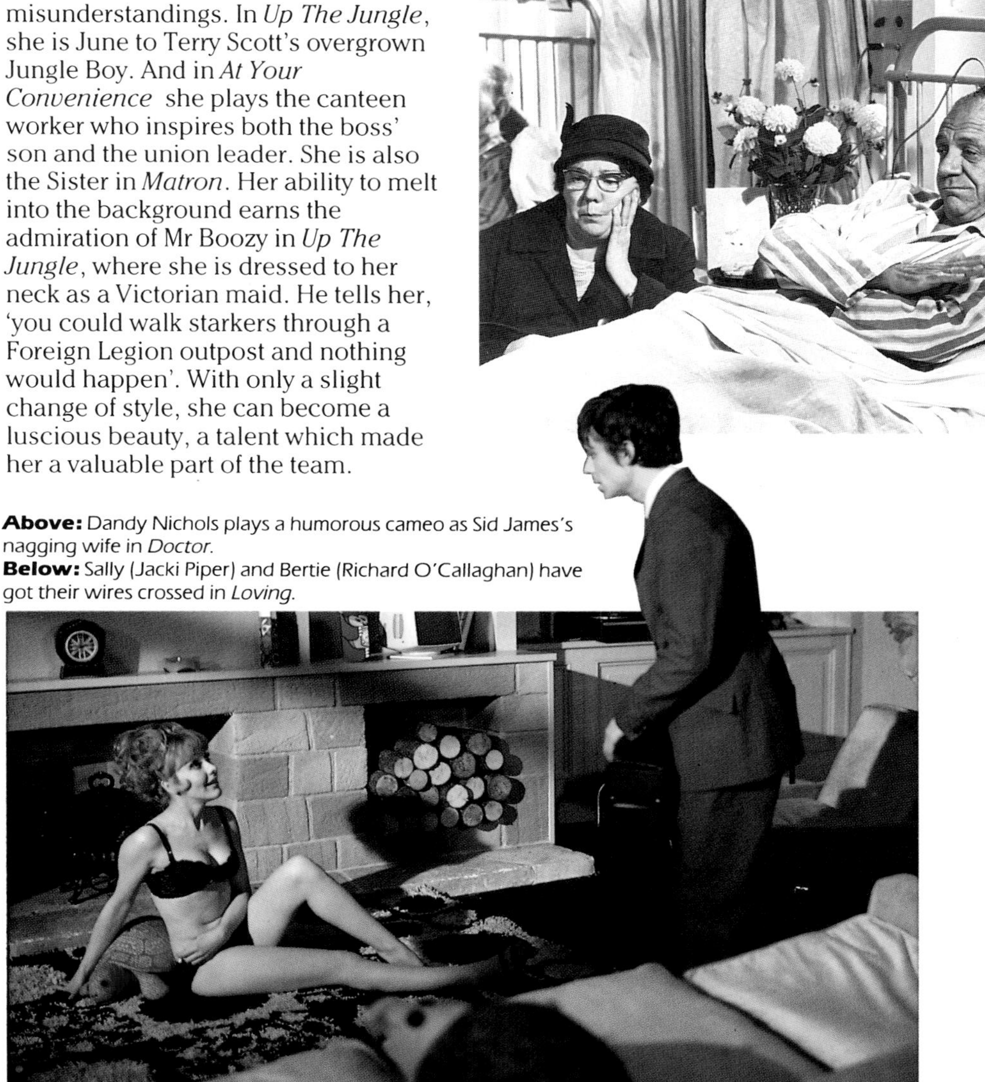

ERIC POHLMANN, the portly Viennese actor renowned for playing sinister villains in crime thrillers, has a small part in *Regardless* as a character in Kenneth Connor's spy fantasy. He also plays The Fat Man, one of Dr Crow's henchmen, in *Spying*.

ADRIENNE POSTA, one of the Sixties' swingers and best-known for her role in *To Sir, With Love* (1967), appears as a camper, Norma Baxter, in *Behind*.

ROBIN RAY, the son of Ted Ray and now a TV personality who hosts *Film Buff of the Year* and his own music show, appears as a shop manager, baffled by two coppers in drag, in *Constable*.

TED RAY was a top-line music hall and radio comedian who played the violin as part of his act. He took several straight parts in British films and plays the lead as the respected headmaster in *Teacher*. He gives the part an easy charm which neatly complements the skills of the Carry On team. He died in 1977.

BERYL REID, the celebrated comedienne and character actress – memorable as the soap opera star in *The Killing of Sister George* (1969) – plays Mrs Valentine, the over-protective mother of the odious Theodore in *Emmannuelle*. She later won much acclaim for her performance as Connie in the TV dramatization of the John Le Carré novel *Tinker, Tailor, Soldier, Spy.*

EVA REUBER-STAIER, the 1969 Miss World, is one of Madame Desirée's Birds of Paradise in *Dick*.

WENDY RICHARD plays the shapely contestant Ida Downs – inevitably from Bristol – in *Girls*. She later achieved fame in the TV comedy series *Are You Being Served?* and now plays Pauline Fowler in *EastEnders*. She also appears as the aptly-named, pregnant Nurse Willing in *Matron*.

ARNOLD RIDLEY, the author of the stage and film comedy-thriller *The Ghost Train* and the incontinent Home Guard private in TV's *Dad's Army*, can be seen as Councillor Pratt in *Girls*.

DANY ROBIN, a French actress who has starred in numerous international films including Alfred Hitchcock's *Topaz* (1969), plays Jacqueline the Black Fingernail's girlfriend in *Don't Lose Your Head.*

CARDEW ROBINSON, a TV personality who was The Cad in *The Gang Show*, contributes a remarkable cameo to *Up The Khyber* as the Fakir who entertains the Khazi with his magic but ends his days with his head served on a platter at the famous banquet.

ANTON RODGERS, an accomplished all-round actor who stars in TV's *Fresh Fields* with Julia Mackenzie, appears as a young passenger in *Cruising* and has a more cheeky part in *Jack* as Hardy, the recipient of Nelson's deathbed proposition.

Above: Ted Ray guest stars as the headmaster in *Teacher*, seen here enthusing to Mr Adams (Kenneth Connor).
Left: Phil Silvers joins the Foreign Legion for *Follow That Camel.*
Below: Stanley Unwin as the landlord in *Regardless.*
Right: Sid James chats up Wendy Richard in *Girls.*

NORMAN ROSSINGTON has been in many film and TV series, including *The Army Game* in which he played Sergeant Cupcake and *Curry and Chips* which cast him as a bigoted shop steward. In *Sergeant*, he plays Herbert Brown, the private who keeps failing to pass out. In *Nurse*, he is Norm, running errands up and down the corridors. In *Regardless*, he makes his final Carry On appearance as the referee of a bizarre boxing match in which Charles Hawtrey take his chances in the ring.

PHIL SILVERS, who plays the wily, boastful Sergeant Nocker in *Follow That Camel*, was a veteran of American vaudeville, best-known in Britain for his role in *A Funny Thing Happened on the Way to the Forum* (1966) and as Sergeant Bilko in *The Phil Silvers Show*. He was brought into the Carry Ons when Rank insisted that the cast should include a leading American comic to boost US sales. It was not a successful experiment. Although Silvers entered into the Carry On spirit on screen, he caused problems during production with his 'star' behaviour and found it difficult to fit into the tight discipline of the Carry On shooting schedule. He died in 1985.

JACK SMETHURST, known as the son-in-law in *For the Love of Ada*, the pugnacious Eddie Booth in *Love Thy Neighbour* and Eddie Yates' fellow binman in *Coronation Street*, is one of the raw recruits in *Sergeant*.

June Whitfield is Councillor Prodworthy, the champion of women's rights, forever baiting the Mayor (Kenneth Connor) in *Girls*.

Professor Anna Vrooshka (Elke Sommer), a talented archaeologist, steps from her caravan in *Behind*.

ELKE SOMMER. Glamorous star of German, Italian, French, American and British films, Elke Sommer is one of the very few international actresses to have featured in a Carry On. As Professor Vrooshka, the Russian archaeologist in *Behind*, she gives a spirited performance, her fractured English adding another dimension to the laugh-lines. Film director Vittorio de Sica introduced her to films when he saw her picture as the winner of a local beauty contest. She has worked in Europe and Hollywood and *Deadlier Than the Male* (1966) ranks among her British films. It was this film that brought her into the Carry On orbit as it was produced by Betty Box, the wife of Carry On producer Peter Rogers.

ELEANOR SUMMERFIELD, who chaired the TV quiz *Password* in the Seventies, had her part in *Regardless* cut out. She is well-known from numerous TV plays.

SIDNEY TAFLER, the suave spiv of many British films, has a cameo in *Regardless* as a club manager looking for bouncers.

FRANK THORNTON, familiar to TV viewers as Captain Peacock in *Are You Being Served?* plays the shop manager who refuses to believe that his window dummies are real women in *Screaming*.

STANLEY UNWIN, the comedian famous for his unique brand of gobbledegook, brings his own language into *Regardless* when he is trying to let the Helping Hands Agency know that he is their landlord.

RICHARD WATTIS who has played every conceivable kind of man from the ministry in countless British films, is – typically – a bureaucrat in *Spying*.

CAROL WHITE, the star of TV's *Cathy Come Home*, whose films include *Circus Friends* (Gerald Thomas' first film in 1956) and *Poor Cow* (1967), is one of the rebel pupils in *Teacher*.

JUNE WHITFIELD's three Carry Ons span almost the entire life of the series. She appears briefly as Leslie Phillips' girlfriend in *Nurse* and plays Evelyn Blunt, the frigid wife who loses her inhibitions through a Spanish romance in *Abroad*. She excels in *Girls* as Councillor Prodworthy, the leader of the Women's Lib group which sabotages the beauty contest and explodes the event to chaos. In her early career, she was teamed with many top-line comedians and was familiar to radio listeners as Eth, Dick Bentley's whingeing girlfriend in *Take It From Here*. Now one of Britain's leading exponents of marital farce, her partnership with Terry Scott in the TV series *Terry On . . .* and *Terry and June* was so convincing it misled many viewers into believing that they were married in real life. She was awarded the OBE in 1985.

Carry On Sergeant

Sergeant Grimshawe, due for retirement, is determined to win the Star Squad prize with his final platoon of National Servicemen but has reckoned without the idiosyncracies of the motley band of layabouts whom he must first lick into shape.

There are plenty of men in uniform but no heroes in *Carry On Sergeant*, a boisterous barrack-room frolic which sends up army life.

Although there were no plans for a series when the film went into production in 1958, it contains several of the characteristic Carry On elements in embryo. Not least, the cast has the typical bounce and brashness which was to bring audiences flocking to the cinemas.

Kenneth Connor as the nail-biting hypochondriac, Horace Strong; Kenneth Williams as a supercilious egghead; Charles Hawtrey as the airy-fairy Private Golightly; and Hattie Jacques as the imperious Medical Officer established the strip-cartoon personalities which were to carry them on and on regardless.

Eric Barker, with a crisp and quirky performance as the Commanding Officer, Shirley Eaton, Bill Owen and Terence Longden went on to make their marks in further Carry Ons.

For Bob Monkhouse as a bridegroom called up on his wedding day, Dora Bryan as a love-lorn NAAFI girl and William Hartnell as the sentimental sergeant, this was a one-off Carry On.

Norman Hudis' script has a smattering of the awful puns that were to drench the later films in deeper and deeper shades of blue. The medical inspection sequence, with the MO putting the hapless Horace through every medical test in the book to make him face up to reality, gives a foretaste of the wilder anarchy to come.

Captain Clark, the Medical Officer (Hattie Jacques), has an uphill battle to prove to the hypochondriacal and inaptly named Horace Strong (Kenneth Connor) that his body is in peak physical condition.

As a whole, though, *Carry On Sergeant* does not kick over the traces. It is on too tight a rein and its cosy, affectionate attitude to the Army, with officers and squaddies all-pals-together at the end, belongs to an older tradition of British screen comedy.

Made on a shoestring, *Carry on Sergeant* was one of the box-office successes of the year. There had to be a sequel.

Horace (Kenneth Connor) consoles his comrade-at-arms (Monkhouse) who has been called up on his wedding day.

William Hartnell	Sergeant Grimshawe
Bob Monkhouse	Charlie Sage
Shirley Eaton	Mary
Eric Barker	Captain Potts
Dora Bryan	Nora
Bill Owen	Corporal Copping
Charles Hawtrey	Peter Golightly
Kenneth Connor	Horace Strong
Kenneth Williams	James Bailey
Terence Longden	Miles Heywood
Hattie Jacques	Captain Clark (Medical Officer)
Terry Scott	Sergeant O'Brien

Also starred:

Cyril Chamberlain, Frank Forsyth, Basil Dignam, Edward Judd, Anthony Sagar, Jack Smethurst, Partrick Durkin, James Villiers, Henry Livings and Norman Rossington.

Producer	Peter Rogers
Director	Gerald Thomas
Screenplay	Norman Hudis (From *The Bull Boys* by R. F. Delderfield)
Additional material	John Antrobus
Music	Bruce Montgomery
Cinematographer	Peter Hennessy
Editor	Peter Boita

83 min. Black and white. 1958. Cert. U.

Privates Brown and Bailey (Norman Rossington and Kenneth Williams) engage in bayonet practice, Carry On style.

Below: bustling and efficient Nurse Denton (Shirley Eaton) has more than medical problems on her mind when she tends appendicitis patient Ted York (Terence Longden). Eaton and Longden provide the romantic interest in this Carry On film and provoke a continual 'will they, won't they?' sub-plot.

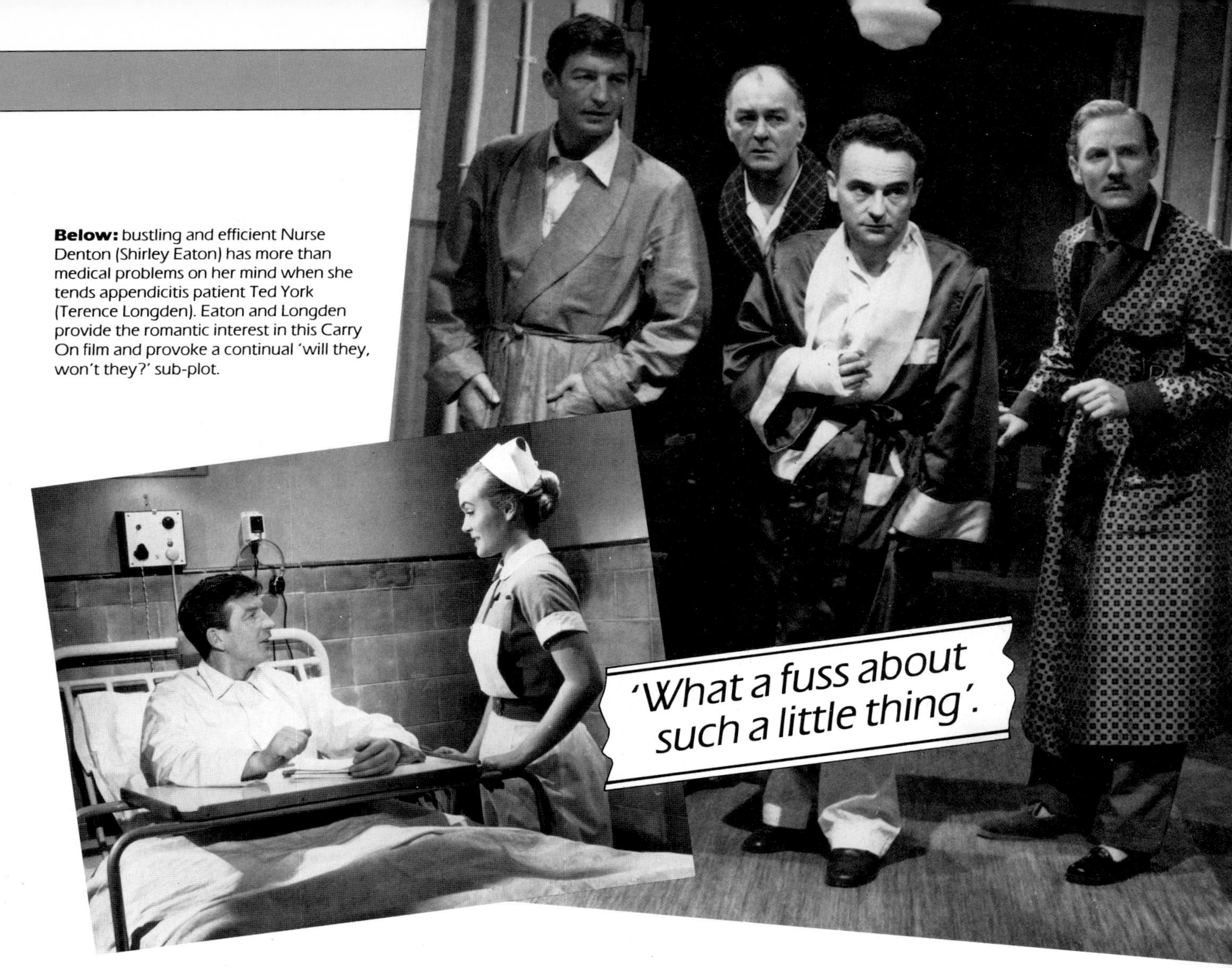

Carry On Nurse

The patients of the men's surgical ward of Haven Hospital create their own peculiar brand of havoc which reaches its peak when they decide to embark on a secret, midnight, do-it-yourself operation.

The strict regime of a hospital with its severe nurses, uppity doctors and bullied patients has long been a sitting target for comedy. What was new about *Carry On Nurse* was that its centre of interest was not so much the hospital hierarchy as the patients and nurses. Its phenomenal success at home and in America made a third Carry On inevitable.

Among the patients of Haven Hospital are Bernie Bishop (Kenneth Connor), a jaunty little boxer with a broken fist and a bleeding heart, and Mr Hinton (Charles Hawtrey) who spends almost the entire film locked into his radio earphones. Percy Hickson (Bill Owen), with his plastered leg slung up with ropes and pulleys, would give anything for a bit of peace – or a bottle – while his wife (Irene Handl in a delightful cameo) bores him to tears with details of his insurance claim. Jack Bell (Leslie Phillips) is desperate to have a painful bunion removed before embarking upon a long-planned romantic rendezvous (with June Whitfield). Guest star Wilfrid Hyde-White plays the Colonel, an obstreperous private patient – 'a naughty old buzzer' – who drives the nurses wild with his constant demands to be kept in touch with his bookmaker.

Among the nurses, Shirley Eaton as Dorothy Denton provides the glamour and romance, a very young-looking Joan Sims is a disaster-prone probationer and Matron, Hattie Jacques, regularly does her rounds.

The targets were the rotten food and formidable discipline. Matron billows along the corridors and wards like a ship in full sail, sending out shock waves of disapproval and retribution to everyone in her path.

Kenneth Williams, as Oliver Reckitt, a priggish nuclear physics student, is the only one to stand up to her – with a few choice words which sum up everyone's self-assertion fantasy.

Climax of the action is a midnight rendezvous in the operating theatre, but the laughter climax comes in the closing minutes of the film. Two young nurses, taking their revenge on the Colonel, set up the celebrated daffodil joke. Matron arrives in the private ward to find that the nurses have turned him on his front to have his temperature taken in a private place. She looks outraged. 'Come, come, Matron,' he says from his prostrate position, 'surely you've seen a temperature taken like this before?'

'Yes, Colonel,' she replies in her frostiest tones, 'many times. But never with a daffodil!'

The patients of the King George V men's surgical ward are on the warpath to take their revenge on the hospital hierarchy. They are (from left to right) Ted (Terence Longden), Bert (Cyril Chamberlain), Bernie (Kenneth Connor), Jack (Leslie Phillips) and Oliver (Kenneth Williams).

PRODUCER'S NOTE

Just as *Carry On Sergeant* had been fashioned from a dramatic subject, *The Bull Boys*, the sequel came out of another dramatic subject, a play called 'Ring For Catty'. This was a drama set in a TB sanatorium. When Stuart Levy and I were discussing a sequel to *Carry On Sergeant* I suggested a film about a hospital and nurses. Knowing that I owned the play, Stuart exclaimed, 'Not that "Ring for Catty"?' I said no, it wouldn't be 'Ring for Catty'. It would be called *Carry On Nurse* and only loosely based on the play. Stuart gave the go ahead and *Carry On Nurse* was born, fully financed by the National Film Finance Corporation and distributed, as in the case of *Carry On Sergeant*, by Anglo Amalgamated.

This film turned out to be Number One in the box office poll, and on the strength of the two Carry Ons I was offered a five-film contract by Anglo Amalgamated. Other producers suggested that I could now write my own ticket and tackle any subject I liked. I said, 'No thanks. I'd rather stay in my own back yard'. I've been pottering around there ever since.

Hattie Jacques, in her most typical Carry On role, beams benignly at the famous daffodil in the final sketch of the film. Despite her frosty 'Queen Victoria' image, matron proves that even she can be amused when a particularly difficult patient gets his due comeuppance.

Shirley Eaton	Dorothy Denton
Kenneth Connor	Bernie Bishop
Charles Hawtrey	Hinton
Hattie Jacques	Matron
Terence Longden	Ted York
Bill Owen	Percy Hickson
Leslie Phillips	Jack Bell
Joan Sims	Stella Dawson
Kenneth Williams	Oliver Reckitt
(Guest Star) **Wilfrid Hyde-White**	The Colonel

Also starred:
Susan Stephen, Susan Beaumont, Norman Rossington, Jill Ireland, Joan Hickson, Irene Handl, Susan Shaw, Michael Medwin (Guest appearance), Cyril Chamberlain, June Whitfield, Frank Forsyth, Rosalind Knight, Hilda Fenemore, Ed Devereaux and Anthony Sagar.

Producer	Peter Rogers
Director	Gerald Thomas
Screenplay	Norman Hudis

Based on an idea by Patrick Cargill and Jack Searle

Music	Bruce Montgomery
Cinematographer	Reg Wyer
Editor	John Shirley

86 min. Black and White. 1959. Cert. U.

Carry On Teacher

The pupils of Maudlin Street School lace the staff tea with alcohol, saw through the legs of the grand piano, dowse the headmaster's study with itching powder and stage an elaborate bomb scare – all in the cause of sabotaging their headmaster's application for a new post, so that they can keep him for themselves.

To cane or not to cane? That was the question confronting not only the educationalists of the late Fifties but also the motley assortment of staff who carry on teaching at Maudlin Street School. On the side of discipline are the forbidding maths teacher (Hattie Jacques in mortar board and gown) the shapely gym mistress (Joan Sims) and the sour-faced woman from the Ministry (Rosalind Knight). The softer option is supported by the drama teacher (Kenneth Williams, in an unusually liberal role) who has the best line on the issue – 'extraordinary theory! You bend a child double in order to give him an upright character'. His ally is a 'namby-pamby, starry-eyed, head-shrinker' (Leslie Phillips) who argues the case for free discipline and the extremely popular headmaster (Ted Ray in his one and only Carry On who, incidentally, went on to make other films with Peter Rogers and Gerald Thomas).

When the head decides to apply for an important new post, the kids take action. They are led by Robin Stevens, played by a very young Richard O'Sullivan who became known to a later generation through TV's *Robin's Nest* and *Me and My Girl*. They get up to all sorts of pranks to blacken the head's reputation with Miss Wheeler, the woman from the Ministry, to ensure he cannot get another job and will therefore have to stay with the school.

The saucy dialogue – now an essential part of the proceedings – flows from the staff-room romances, with the passionate psychologist chasing the no-nonsense gym mistress, and nervous little Mr Adams (Kenneth Connor) falling for the formidable Miss Wheeler.

PRODUCER'S NOTE

Ted Ray was replaced in the Rogers-Thomas comedies by Sid James. The story behind this is as follows.

Anglo Amalgamated were distributors, without their own cinema circuit in which to release their films. So they had a working arrangement with Associated British (ABC, later to become EMI, later to become Cannon, later to become Weintraub). Ted Ray had been under contract to ABC for several years but had never been given a film. Consequently ABC were more than embarrassed to see an ex-contract and unused star of theirs turning up in someone else's films – and most successfully. This feeling was passed on to Stuart Levy, with a request to ask me to drop Ted Ray. I was thunderstruck and inclined to tell ABC to go the devil, and their casting director with them. But Stuart explained that it could mean the difference between release and non-release of the films. Whether or not such a situation would have arisen if I had refused Stuart's request, the fact remained that the Amalgamated directors and the ABC directors were all great buddies in the Variety Club of Great Britain. I acceded to Stuart's request. Ted Ray never knew why he was dropped. I never told him because I felt that complicated lawsuits might ensue. Ted Ray was one of the very nicest people we ever worked with.

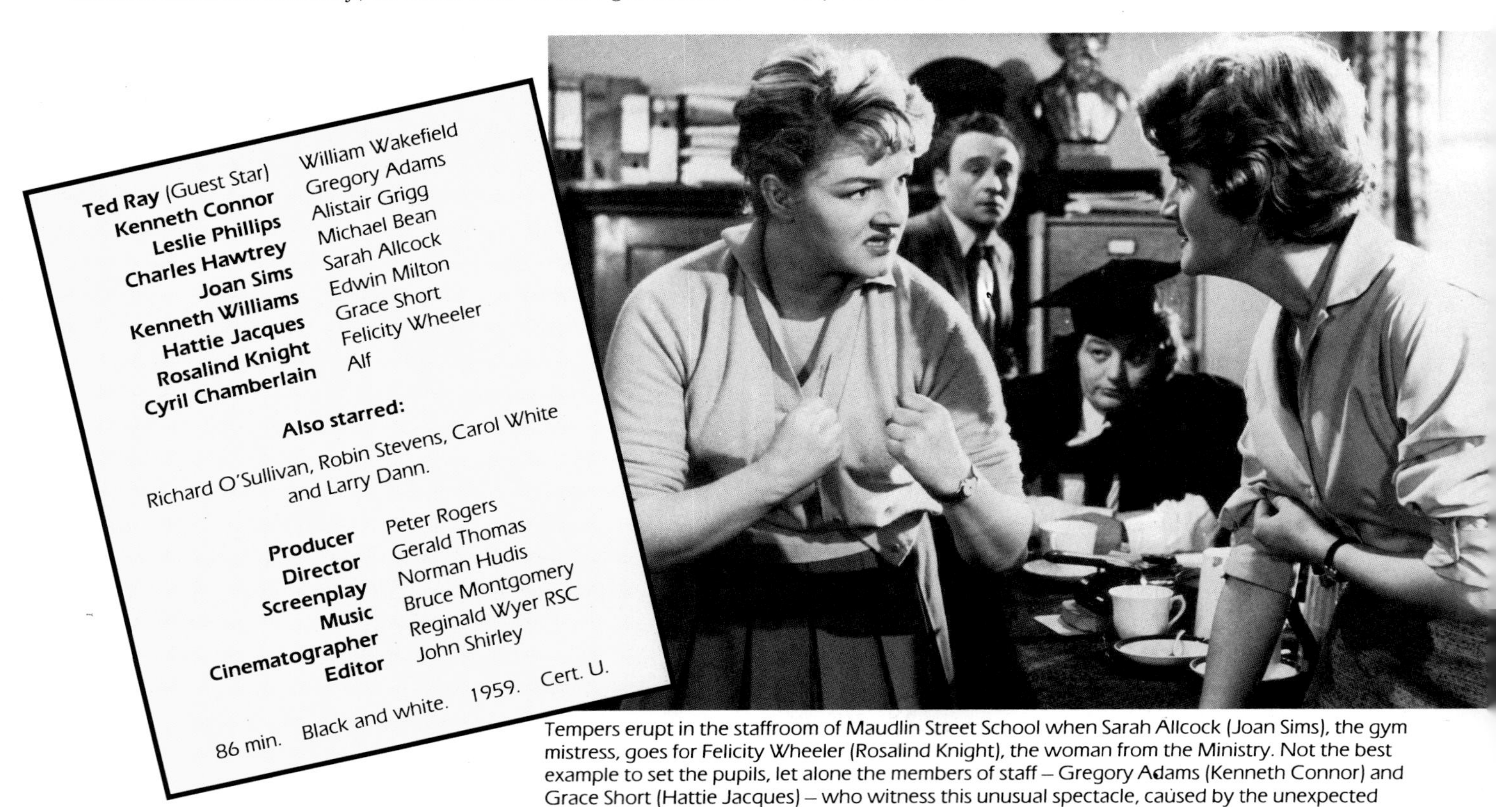

Ted Ray (Guest Star)	William Wakefield
Kenneth Connor	Gregory Adams
Leslie Phillips	Alistair Grigg
Charles Hawtrey	Michael Bean
Joan Sims	Sarah Allcock
Kenneth Williams	Edwin Milton
Hattie Jacques	Grace Short
Rosalind Knight	Felicity Wheeler
Cyril Chamberlain	Alf

Also starred:

Richard O'Sullivan, Robin Stevens, Carol White and Larry Dann.

Producer	Peter Rogers
Director	Gerald Thomas
Screenplay	Norman Hudis
Music	Bruce Montgomery
Cinematographer	Reginald Wyer RSC
Editor	John Shirley

86 min. Black and white. 1959. Cert. U.

Tempers erupt in the staffroom of Maudlin Street School when Sarah Allcock (Joan Sims), the gym mistress, goes for Felicity Wheeler (Rosalind Knight), the woman from the Ministry. Not the best example to set the pupils, let alone the members of staff – Gregory Adams (Kenneth Connor) and Grace Short (Hattie Jacques) – who witness this unusual spectacle, caused by the unexpected presence of alcohol in the staff tea.

Fun and games in the showers of the local cop shop when the three new recruits to the force – Constable Porter (Leslie Phillips), Constable Benson (Kenneth Williams) and the aptly-named Constable Constable (Kenneth Connor) – are surprised at their ablutions by a female presence.

Sidney James	Sgt Frank Wilkins
Eric Barker	Inspector Mills
Kenneth Connor	Constable Charlie Constable
Charles Hawtrey	Special Constable Gorse
Kenneth Williams	Constable Benson
Leslie Phillips	Constable Porter
Joan Sims	Policewoman Gloria Passworthy
Hattie Jacques	Sgt Laura Moon
Shirley Eaton	Sally
Cyril Chamberlain	Constable Thurston

Also starred:

Joan Hickson, Irene Handl, Terence Longden, Jill Adams, Freddie Mills, Victor Maddern, Esma Cannon, Hilda Fenemore, Frank Forsyth, John Antrobus and Robin Ray.

Producer	Peter Rogers
Director	Gerald Thomas
Screenplay	Norman Hudis

Based on an idea by Brock Williams

Music	Bruce Montgomery
Cinematographer	Ted Scaife RSC
Editor	John Shirley

86 min. Black and white. 1960. Cert. U.

Carry On Constable

Four trainee policemen arrive as reinforcements at the local nick and bungle their duties with some very off-beat practices.

In 1960, millions of televiewers settled down each week for their regular fix of *Dixon of Dock Green*. This Carry On, set at a local police station, puts its size eleven boot through the smug reassurance of the TV series in a riotous send-up of your friendly neighbourhood bobby.

Sid James enters the Carry On fray for the first time as Sergeant Wilkins, who has to lick an unlikely selection of newcomers into shape. They are: Constable Potter (Leslie Phillips), known as 'potty poodles' to his debby friends, who arrives for duty with his tennis racquet under his arm; Constable Benson (Kenneth Williams), 'a born mug' who holds advanced theories on forensic physiognomy and who is given to such pompous utterances as 'your misreading of my potential is sublime in its totality'; superstitious Constable Constable (Kenneth Connor) who cannot even fall in love without checking the astrology charts; and Special Constable Gorse (Charles Hawtrey) whose gay heartiness leads to memorable statements like: 'I haven't done this since the Army when I was in a camp concert'. Completing the picture is WPC Passworthy (Joan Sims) who, unlike her colleagues, is rather good at her job.

There's a quickfire succession of small comic incidents as each of the rookies takes his turn on the beat. Dogs run amok, old women are harassed, robbers are aided and abetted, while the general public are perplexed. In the now traditional drag sequence, PCs Benson and Gorse, dressed as Agatha and a rather attractive Ethel, patrol a big store on the track of shoplifters, but contrive to get themselves arrested.

But all's well that ends well, as the infamous four join forces to arrest a notorious wage-snatching gang, leading to one of scriptwriter Norman Hudis' happy, all-is-forgiven endings.

PRODUCER'S NOTE

For this film Norman Hudis was sent to Slough police station for a week to study police procedure. In fact he became so close to the situations at the station that he confessed to me that he couldn't see any comedy in it. So I said forget it, start work on another subject and go back to 'Constable' later. And that is how *Carry On Constable* became the comedy it was.

Sid James makes his first appearance in a Carry On as the long-suffering Sergeant Williams bedevilled by three calamitous constables sent along to plug the gaps in his flu-decimated roster. With Phillips, Connor and Williams on the beat, thieves have a field day while no innocent bystander is safe from their attentions.

Carry On Regardless

Six unemployed men and women and the counter clerk from the employment exchange go in search of adventure and excitement by joining the Helping Hands agency, where the staff are sent out on some very odd jobs and the left Hand seldom knows what the right Hand is doing.

This bumper Carry On is a little different from the others. It is essentially a series of comic sketches built around separate assignments as the Helping Hands agency (run by Sidney James and Esma Cannon) takes on new tasks. Its clients include a galaxy of well-known comedy and character players.

Sidney James	Bert Handy (Proprietor)
Kenneth Connor	Sam Twist
Charles Hawtrey	Gabriel Dimple
Joan Sims	Lily Duveen
Kenneth Williams	Francis Courtenay
Bill Owen	Mike Weston
Liz Fraser	Delia King
Terence Longden	Montgomery Infield-Hopping
Esma Cannon	Miss Cooling (Assistant)

Also starred:

Hattie Jacques, Sidney Tafler, Julia Arnall, Terence Alexander, Stanley Unwin, Joan Hickson, Betty Marsden, Fenella Fielding, David Lodge, Jerry Desmonde, Ambrosine Phillpotts, Nicholas Parsons, Cyril Chamberlain, Eric Pohlmann, Judith Furse, Howard Marion Crawford, Freddie Mills, Norman Rossington, Patrick Cargill, Ed Devereaux and Victor Maddern.

Producer	Peter Rogers
Director	Ralph Thomas
Screenplay	Norman Hudis
Music	Bruce Montgomery
Cinematographer	Alan Hume RSC
Editor	John Shirley

90 min. Black and white. 1960. Cert. U.

Fenella Fielding says she wants a baby-sitter; Nicholas Parsons and Patrick Cargill are at a wine-tasting; Joan Hickson and Hattie Jacques turn up at the local hospital (where else?); Sidney Tafler needs a bouncer; and Freddie Mills is a boxing promoter looking for seconds. Given the chance, Helping Hands agency can reduce even the simplest assignment to chaos.

Sam Twist (Kenneth Connor) gets a garbled phone message and ends up searching for a rendezvous on the Forth Bridge in nervous imitation of Richard Hannay. He's got it wrong – he was supposed to be providing a fourth at bridge. Multi-lingual Francis Courtenay (Kenneth Williams) is sent to interpret an argument betwen Mr Trelawney (Terence Alexander) and his wife (Julia Arnall) who is so angry she has lapsed into her native German.

All the staff join forces for a rumbustious slapstick sequence when they are hired as demonstrators at the Ideal Home Exhibition. Everything from vacuum cleaners to toys gets out of control in their Hands. And when an office spring-clean leads to an assignment mix-up, the various strands get tangled together.

Popping in and out of the Helping Hands office is Stanley Unwin, who baffles everyone with his unique brand of gobbledegook. They finally realize that he is their landlord and he wants them out. But he changes his mind when the team inadvertently do him a favour by ruining one of his properties instead of cleaning it up thereby enhancing the land value. What else can they do but carry on regardless?

Above: Delia (Liz Fraser) has to do some quick thinking when she is caught in a client's bedroom and his wife returns.

Left: Francis Courtenay (Kenneth Williams), speaker of sixteen languages, finds work taking a monkey for a walk.

The **SS Happy Wanderer** in **Carry On Cruising** never went to sea. It was a full-scale replica of a cruise-liner, complete with cabins, swimming-pools, bars and deck games, designed by art director Carmen Dillon, and constructed at Pinewood by studio craftsmen.

Dr Binn (Kenneth Connor) and First Officer Marjoribanks (Kenneth Williams) have a painful cure for seasickness which Chef Wilfred Haines (Lance Percival) fails to appreciate.

Sidney James	*Captain Crowther*
Kenneth Williams	*Leonard Marjoribanks*
Kenneth Connor	*Arthur Binn*
Liz Fraser	*Glad Trimble*
Dilys Laye	*Flo Castle*
Esma Cannon	*Bridget Madderley*
Lance Percival	*Wilfred Haines*

Also starred:

Jimmy Thompson, Ronnie Stevens, Vincent Ball, Cyril Chamberlain, Ed Devereaux, Anthony Sagar and Anton Rodgers.

Producer	*Peter Rogers*
Director	*Gerald Thomas*
Screenplay	*Norman Hudis*
From a story by	*Eric Barker*
Music	*Bruce Montgomery and Douglas Gamley*
Cinematographer	*Alan Hume RSC*
Editor	*John Shirley*

89 min. Eastman Color. 1962. Cert. U.

Carry On Cruising

The passengers and crew of a Mediterranean cruise ship dress up or throw up, play deck games or power games, get drunk or misunderstood, and fall in love or out of deckchairs.

Carry On Cruising was the first of the series in colour and the last to be scripted by Norman Hudis. Like all of its predecessors, it starts with a conflict and ends in togetherness.

In *Cruising* the conflict is set up between the insecure H-dropping Captain Crowther (Sidney James) and five eager-beaver crew replacements whose arrival plays havoc with the ship's routine and the Captain's fragile peace of mind.

Among the unwelcome newcomers are Kenneth Williams as the snooty First Officer, Kenneth Connor as the twitchy little ship's doctor, and Lance Percival, in fine form in his only Carry On, as a seasick chef with an unorthodox approach to the art of cooking.

Passengers Dilys Laye as Flo and Liz Fraser as her friend Gladys are on a husband-hunting spree, while Ronnie Stevens wanders in and out of the action in a perpetual alcoholic haze. Esma Cannon steals every scene in which she appears as a twittering, bird-like little passenger ('a mad pixie', according to the Captain) happily entering into the spirit of all the fun and games.

Hudis's traditional 'togetherness' ending is engineered when Connor, having secretly serenaded Flo, finally plucks up courage to declare his love for her; and when the newcomers, having at last earned the Captain's praise, involve everyone in celebrating his tenth year at sea.

Below: two of the lovely, leggy Glamcab girls give an unexpected watery welcome to the male taxi drivers who are trying to sabotage their business by wreaking havoc at their premises. Will a thorough hosing-down dampen the men's ardour in the taxi war between the two firms?

Above: Kenneth Connor takes to drag as a Speedee cabman brazenly trying to infiltrate the opposition's headquarters right in front of Flo (Esma Cannon).

Sidney James	Charlie
Hattie Jacques	Peggy
Kenneth Connor	Ted
Charles Hawtrey	Pint-Pot
Esma Cannon	Flo
Liz Fraser	Sally
Bill Owen	Smiley
Milo O'Shea	Len

Also starred:

Judith Furse, Ambrosine Phillpotts, Renee Houston, Jim Dale, Amanda Barrie, Cyril Chamberlain, Peter Gilmore, Peter Byrne and Frank Forsyth.

Producer	Peter Rogers
Director	Gerald Thomas
Screenplay	Talbot Rothwell
Music	Eric Rogers
Cinematographer	Alan Hume RSC
Editor	Archie Ludski

91 min. Black and white. 1963. Cert. U.

Carry On Cabby

Open warfare is declared between two rival taxi firms when Peggy, neglected by her workaholic husband Charlie, owner of Speedee Taxis, secretly sets up Glamcabs, with gleaming white cars and glamorous women drivers, and steals all his business.

Although it was not originally intended for the series (it was planned as *Call Me a Cab*, which is the last line in the film), it turned out to be a definitive Carry On with all the basic ingredients (but minus Kenneth Williams) in glorious disarray. It has a little extra something too – a comic line in women's self-assertion which finds Charlie (played by Sidney James) anticipating the feminist jargon of the Eighties. 'Blimmin wimmin', he groans.

For Peggy (Hattie Jacques, with an endearing mix of spunk, pathos and humour) the last straw is Charlie's failure to show up for their wedding anniversary spree. Charlie, whose team of cabbies includes Charles Hawtrey, Bill Owen, Kenneth Connor and Milo O'Shea, is out on the road. He has been waylaid by an agitated expectant father (Jim Dale playing a tiny but effective part in his first Carry On). High hopes alternate with false alarms as the cab whisks the parents-to-be backwards and forwards between house and hospital – until, finally, the baby is born in the back of the cab.

To exact her revenge, Peggy secretly sets up the highly competitive Glamcabs business, with Flo (Esma Cannon), a battling and chirpy old age pensioner, as her right-hand woman; Amanda Barrie, in her first Carry On, among her team of leggy drivers; and Liz Fraser, a mole among the men. Thus begins the Battle of the Taxis.

The anarchic peak of the film is the assault on the Glamcab yard by the Speedee men, with Ted (Connor) disguised as a Glamcab driver, sent ahead to penetrate their defences. But he loses his nerve – and potentially his cover – when faced with the prospect of the women's changing-room.

In the rip-roaring climactic chase, Peggy's cab is hijacked on its way to the bank. Charlie mobilizes all his drivers on the intercom. They give chase, block off all possible getaway streets and finally encircle the stolen cab in the middle of a field in the time-honoured Western tradition.

Above: the glamorous Glamcab drivers have a novel way of dealing with vehicle breakdowns – for not even the most harassed (male) client minds waiting while the gorgeous girls look for willing hands to sort out their mechanical failures. No wonder the male-dominated Speedee cabs are in trouble!

Left: Peggy (Hattie Jacques) and Flo (Esma Cannon) inspect their troops before preparing for action – sending their fleet of cars (and, of course, their delicious drivers armed with good looks and long legs) on to the streets to do battle with the more traditional cabs of the Speedee men.

Carry On Jack

Bernard Cribbins	Albert
Juliet Mills	Sally
Charles Hawtrey	Walter
Kenneth Williams	Captain Fearless
Donald Houston	Howett
Percy Herbert	Angel
Peter Gilmore	Patch

Also starred:

Ed Devereaux, Jim Dale, Ian Wilson, Barrie Gosney, Cecil Parker, Frank Forsyth, Anton Rodgers and Patrick Cargill.

Uncredited:
Dorinda Stephens, Sally Douglas and Dominique Don.

Producer	Peter Rogers
Director	Gerald Thomas
Screenplay	Talbot Rothwell
Music	Eric Rogers
Cinematographer	Alan Hume RSC
Editor	Archie Ludski

91 min. Eastman Color. 1964. Cert. A.

Nelson makes his improper suggestion to Hardy; Sally becomes an improper member of the crew of the frigate *Venus*; Albert Poop-Decker makes improper advances to her; and there is nothing at all proper about Captain Fearless.

The successful use of colour in *Carry On Cruising* opened out a new world for the Carry Ons. If in colour, why not in costume? If in costume, then the whole of history was theirs to plunder. So began a new phase of the Carry Ons – the hysterical historicals.

The British Navy, that good old faithful of many a screen epic from the swashbuckling days of Errol Flynn to the later remake of *Mutiny on the Bounty* (1962), was a perfect starting point.

With few of the Carry On regulars present, this is Bernard Cribbins' film. He stars as Albert Poop-Decker, a greenhorn young gent, newly commissioned as a Midshipman after eight-and-a-half years of failing to pass out. It is Albert who falls for Sally (Juliet Mills in her only Carry On) although she has stolen his uniform, impersonated him and taken his place on the *Venus*. Albert is the special target of the fearsome Bligh-like First Officer (Donald Houston) and equally daunting bosun (Percy Herbert), forever stapping their vitals. It is Albert who befriends the press-ganged cesspit cleaner Walter (Charles Hawtrey); and Albert who mollycoddles Captain Fearless (Kenneth Williams) – 'if you've got a heart of oak, it's got the worm in it', say the crew.

With the Spanish fleet threatening war and pirates roving the high seas, there is plenty of action and adventure – but always with a Carry On twist. After a mock mutiny, Albert, Sally, Walter and the Captain are cast adrift in a small boat. In the best – or worst – tradition of shipwreck dramas they

Will the real Midshipman Albert Poop-Decker stand up? Sally (Juliet Mills) is dressed for the part (**above**) but only because she has stolen the uniform from Albert (Bernard Cribbins) which is why (**right**) he has to take his punishment in her nightdress.

Above: when the good ship *Venus* is boarded by pirates on the high seas, the captain (Kenneth Williams) is not disposed to put up a fight.

Left: Sally (Juliet Mills) and Walter (Charles Hawtrey) assist Albert (Bernard Cribbins) at an impromptu operation to amputate the captain's foot with an evil-looking set of surgical blades.

almost die of thirst and are planning to eat each other when Albert bravely decides to swim for it. In one of the film's funniest moments he holds his nose, jumps over the side – and finds himself in six inches of water.

The *Venus*'s ultimate victory – the destruction of five Spanish ships (albeit already in British hands) – is sparked off when Walter accidentally sets the frigate alight while heating some water, causing a cataclysmic chain reaction. The four castaways find they are the victors of a battle they never knew they fought.

For all these high and low jinks, the most memorable sequence is at the beginning of the film when wily sedan chair carrier (Jim Dale), and his decrepit old dad (Ian Wilson) take Albert for a ride. In classic Carry On tradition, Albert is conveyed in a bottomless litter with his own legs doing all the work. He is then persuaded that a seedy dockside tavern is the ideal place to meet a nice well-bred young woman and that the local custom is to hold out a gold coin on your entrance. In the resulting stampede it becomes apparent that the Admiralty (in the avuncular shape of Cecil Parker) knew what they were doing when they decreed that Albert would never make a sailor.

PRODUCER'S NOTE

This was the first script submitted to me by Talbot Rothwell. It was originally called 'Up the Armada' but the censor refused to sanction the title in spite of later films such as *Up Pompeii*. I sought Talbot Rothwell's permission to call it 'Carry On Jack'. Although the writer's permission was not necessary, I felt at the time that not every writer wanted to be associated with what the critics called 'fatheaded farce'. 'Up The Armada' became *Carry On Jack* and Talbot Rothwell went on to write another 19 Carry On scripts.

Carry On Spying

Kenneth Williams	Desmond Simpkins
Bernard Cribbins	Harold Crump
Charles Hawtrey	Charlie Bind
Barbara Windsor	Daphne Honeybutt
Eric Pohlmann	The Fat Man
Eric Barker	The Chief
Dilys Laye	Lila
Jim Dale	Carstairs
Richard Wattis	Cobley

Also starred:

Judith Furse, Victor Maddern, Frank Forsyth, Tom Clegg and Renee Houston.

Producer	Peter Rogers
Director	Gerald Thomas
Screenplay	Talbot Rothwell and Sid Colin
Music	Eric Rogers

Songs

'Too Late' Alex Alstone and Geoffrey Parsons
'The Magic of Love' Eric Rogers

Cinematographer	Alan Hume RSC
Editor	Archie Ludski

87 min. Black and white. 1964. Cert. A.

Agent Simpkins and his three trainees pit their wits against The Fat Man, The Milchman and Dr Crow, the evil leader of the Society for the Total Extinction of Non-Conforming Humans, commonly known as STENCH.

This was the Carry On team's excursion into the shadowy world of spies and secrets. This spoof spy adventure romps through the dark streets and silent corners of Vienna; follows its nose to the Casbah where underworld villains drink at street cafés and make midnight assignations; joins the Orient Express on which hoods and beautiful women fight in and out of the corridors; and finally lands at the high-tech headquarters of STENCH, where black-clad men and women guard the controls of a fully-automated plant. This is no ordinary secret service yarn. It is a dyed-in-the-wool Carry On.

All the cinematic references are present and correct. There is a false briefcase containing everything from false passports to false eyelashes and, naturally, made of imitation leather. Concealed radios lurk in everything from cigarette cases to brassieres. There are cunningly disguised entrances to top-secret establishments, the most bizarre being a gents toilet in the middle of a deserted field. There

Above: agents on parade. Richard Wattis and Eric Barker, two regulars of spy films, add their weight to the Carry On secret service.

Left: special agents Crump and Honeybutt (Bernard Cribbins and Barbara Windsor) seek entrance to the inner recesses of the Casbah.

Right: Barbara Windsor's Daphne Honeybutt (code name: Brown Cow) proves she can withstand the most dastardly torture.

are numerous disguises. Jim Dale as Carstairs, our man in Vienna, pops up as a ticket collector, a customs officer, a blind match seller and a prostitute.

On the track of a stolen chemical formula are Agent Simpkins, played by Kenneth Williams – 'I wish the other side would make him an offer', muses his boss; Howard Crump (Bernard Cribbins in his second and last Carry On role); Charlie Bind (Charles Hawtrey), the walking disaster area of the team; and Daphne Honeybutt, played by a newcomer to the Carry Ons, Barbara Windsor. Her debut is an instant winner. From the moment she has difficulty getting her underarm holster to fasten across her celebrated pair of assets it is clear that she is here to stay. Blonde she may be but dumb she ain't. Daphne, code name Brown Cow, is undoubtedly the best agent of them all with her photographic memory, quick thinking responses and ability to withstand even the most dastardly torture. While her colleagues try to protect her as the woman of the team, Daphne is out and about, out-spying them all.

The climax, an hilarious roller-coaster ride on an automated metal factory train, is a fine tribute to James Bond as well as a lot of fun. And even the final, inevitable, destruction of the villains' headquarters has its own unique Carry On twist.

PRODUCER'S NOTE

As soon as it was rumoured that Charlie Bind was going to be known as 001½, Harry Saltzman's lawyer was on the phone, threatening to sue me. He even objected to the name 'Bind' but on this point I was adamant and only discarded the figures 001½.

Carry On Cleo

From an Original Idea By William Shakespeare. Hengist invents the square wheel while Horsa fights Romans, Caesar ignores the Ides of March while Mark Antony takes liberties with Cleopatra and Seneca is a sage who knows his onions.

Above left: the fearless Horsa (Jim Dale) takes his new bride back in the traditional manner to the Stone Age village of Coqium.

Above: Cleo (Amanda Barrie) has her own methods of egging Mark Antony (Sid James) onto bigger and better things.

Right: it is the Ides of March for Caesar (Kenneth Williams), perhaps because he can never remember what comes after 'friends, Romans and . . .'

With the rise of TV and the fall of cinema in the Fifties, the film industry tried to tempt the queues back to the box-office with something TV could not provide: spectacular widescreen epics, culling stories from the Bible, mythology and ancient history. By 1964, Ancient Rome had become familiar territory with films like *Spartacus*, *Ben Hur* and *Julius Caesar*.

The epic to end them all was 20th Century-Fox's disastrous *Cleopatra* (1963), at the time the most expensive film ever made and a financial catastrophe for the studio. It was a sitting target for the Carry On treatment, and when the *Cleopatra* crew decamped to Europe, leaving their sets behind at Pinewood, the opportunity was too good to miss. Amanda Barrie's Cleopatra – a scatterbrained hostess from upper-suburbia – makes its own sly dig at the Elizabeth Taylor version.

The story of Cleopatra is told in homespun Carry On style. Sidney James is a Cockney Mark Antony who betrays his friend and Emperor Julius Caesar (Kenneth Williams who introduces himself with the classic line 'Oh, I do feel queer').

The opening sequence – a Carry On classic – has dreamy little Ancient Briton Hengist Pod (Kenneth Connor) seated outside his dwelling inventing the square wheel (to prevent carts from running backwards downhill) while his cave-proud wife Senna Pod (Sheila Hancock) gets on with the housework all the while haranguing him with a 'working-my-fingers-to-the-bone' monologue which he knows by heart. By the end of the film, the Pods are back at the caveside in blissful mood, surrounded by an array of little Pods.

In between, Hengist has been sold into slavery, condemned to the lion pit, chosen (in mistake for the sword-swinging Horsa) as Caesar's bodyguard, and introduced to Cleopatra's bedchamber in place of his cowardly boss, where he has been given a crash course in the arts of love.

This is one of Kenneth Connor's most engaging roles and Sheila Hancock's Senna – her only *Carry On* role – is a gem of comic timing. Another outstanding one-off appearance comes from Warren Mitchell as the streetwise slave-market auctioneer, Spencius, brother of Marcus.

To provide an atmosphere of mock authenticity, there's an occasional commentary from E V H Emmett, who stresses the film's literary respectability. Cleopatra, he announces in his authentic newsreel voice, was immortalized by Macaulay in his famous poem 'The Lay of Ancient Rome'.

'The eunuchs are on strike. They are complaining about loss of assets'.

Sidney James	Mark Antony
Kenneth Williams	Julius Caesar
Kenneth Connor	Hengist Pod
Charles Hawtrey	Seneca
Joan Sims	Calpurnia
Jim Dale	Horsa
Amanda Barrie	Cleo
EVH Emmett	Narrator

Also starred:

Julie Stevens, Victor Maddern, Sheila Hancock, Tom Clegg, Jon Pertwee, Peter Gilmore and Warren Mitchell.

Producer	Peter Rogers
Director	Gerald Thomas
Screenplay	Talbot Rothwell
Music	Eric Rogers
Cinematographer	Alan Hume RSC
Editor	Archie Ludski

92 min. Eastman Color. 1964. Cert. A.

PRODUCER'S NOTE

Carry On Cleo was involved in a court case over the copyright of the painting of the original 20th Century poster featuring Elizabeth Taylor. The Carry On poster naturally lampooned the famous original with Charles Hawtrey hiding under Cleopatra's bed and suchlike. 20th Century took Anglo Amalgamated to court and won the case. Fortunately Anglo were insured against such a contingency and the resulting publicity was invaluable.

The film incited the threat of another court case. After its press show, one of the critics (I never knew which one) contacted Marks & Spencer not only with the news that their names were bowdlerized as Marcus & Spencius but also that the ribbons adorning the slave trader's booths were the actual colours of M&S – green and gold. The Sieff family passed this information on to their lawyer. Thank God they had an in-house lawyer. Any other lawyer would have gone to town on the case. Once it was explained that no slight to the famous store was intended, the Sieff family settled for a letter of apology and explanation, to be sent to the *Daily Express*. Even this was later dropped and the incident forgotten.

'My name is Belle, but my intimate friends call me Ding Dong'.

Top: The Rumpo Kid (Sid James), the villain of the piece, flirts with the local Belle (Joan Sims) while Charlie (Percy Herbert), the barman, looks on.

Above: Marshall P. Knutt (Jim Dale) finds a novel use for Stodge City's sewers – cover for a gunfight.

Right: Annie (Angela Douglas) and Marshall P. Knutt (Jim Dale) – but mainly Annie – fight off an Indian attack on a stagecoach in Carry On's eventful trip to the Wild West.

Sidney James	The Rumpo Kid
Kenneth Williams	Judge Burke
Joan Sims	Belle
Jim Dale	Marshall P. Knutt
Percy Herbert	Charlie
Angela Douglas	Annie Oakley
Bernard Bresslaw	Little Heap
Charles Hawtrey	Big Heap
Peter Butterworth	Doc

Also starred:

Davy Kaye, Sydney Bromley, Sally Douglas, Jon Pertwee, Peter Gilmore, Brian Rawlinson, Margaret Nolan, Tom Clegg and The Ballet Montparnasse.

Producer	Peter Rogers
Director	Gerald Thomas
Screenplay	Talbot Rothwell
Music	Eric Rogers

Song

'This is the Time for Love' Alan Rogers

Cinematographer	Alan Hume RSC
Editor	Rod Keys

95 min. Eastman Color. 1965. Cert. A.

Above: Annie Oakley (Angela Douglas) tries to train Marshall P. Knutt (Jim Dale) to shoot. It is a difficult task – Mr Knutt is really the local sanitation officer who has found himself wearing a sheriff's badge in a typical case of mistaken identity.

Carry On Cowboy

The Rumpo Kid rides into Stodge City and terrorizes the community, aided by his band of roughnecks and layabouts, until Marshall P Knutt, a keen and conscientious sanitary engineer, is mistaken for a law marshal. With a helping hand from revenge-seeking Annie Oakley, he proves in the final shoot-out that there is more to drains than dirty water.

This is one of the most ambitious Carry Ons with a big cast and an unexpected change in acting style. Instead of the gang pretending to be dressed-up Westerners, in the usual Carry On tradition, this time they play it for real. Gone are the Cockney accents and the mock-refined voices. Everyone talks the American way, though the dialogue is still pure Carry On – 'I'm from Texas, we've all got big ones down there'.

Kenneth Williams, as the elderly Judge Burke, has his mobile face largely hidden by greying sideburns and moustache. The production team, keen to get the detail authentic, had brought in experts to teach Western-style riding, and Sid James plays the Rumpo Kid as if to the saddle born.

The film opens with a 'cross-the-wide-prairie' song, written by the series resident composer Eric Rogers. Annie Oakley's song, 'This is the Time for Love', was written by his brother Alan Rogers.

PRODUCER'S NOTE

I wanted Charles Hawtrey, as the Indian Chief, to sing a snatch of a song from Rose Marie – 'When I'm calling you, Double O, Double O' – but the American company which owns the rights would not play ball.

Also in this film, you see for the first time a Western main street with a right hand turn at the end of it. This was done to hide the fact that there was no wild prairie on the Pinewood lot.

You also see the Stage Coach racing across open country near Esher in Surrey with dust flying up from the wheels. This was provided by a property man sitting in the coach with a powder gun – in spite of the fact that the horses were kicking up mud. It was one of the wettest days on location.

Carry On Screaming

Detective-Sergeant Bung, accompanied by his assistant Slobotham, investigates the sudden disappearance of Doris and comes face to face with the bloodcurdling experiments organized by the mysterious Dr Watt and his siren sister Valeria who are vitrifying young women to sell to local stores as shop-window dummies.

The Hammer Horrors had been going strong for ten years when the *Carry On* team sank their teeth into the subject, biting chunks out of all the gruesome goings-on which had haunted the cinema from its earliest days.

Harry H Corbett, in Sherlock Holmes cape and deerstalker, plays the earnest, thickheaded Detective-Sergeant Bung, his only *Carry On* role. Creaking doors, a sinister butler (Bernard Bresslaw), a mummy brought to life, a potion (lent by Dr Jekyll) which transforms men into hairy beasts, monsters impervious to bullets – these are just a few of the clues he fails to grasp. Only when the vitrified Doris (Angela Douglas) is discovered are his suspicions aroused. 'There's something funny going on in this house', he confides to her anxious boyfriend Alan (Jim Dale).

Kenneth Williams, with dead-white face and sunken eyes, plays the undead Dr Watt who, as the special effects department vividly illustrates, will disintegrate if he isn't plugged into the mains at regular intervals. Fenella Fielding as Valeria – her second *Carry On* role – is more of a vamp than a vampire, but when Detective-Constable Slobotham (Peter Butterworth), falls into their hands, it is she who suggests driving a stake through his heart. 'No', says Dr Watt peevishly, 'I don't feel like driving tonight'.

The show is stolen by the two monsters: the massively four-square Odbodd (Tom Clegg); and his offspring, Odbodd Junior (Billy Cornelius) who, in memory of the original Frankenstein's monster, played by Boris Karloff in the 1931 Hollywood classic, has an engaging childlike charm.

The Carry Ons often feature musical jokes and there are many which provoke a grin of recognition in this one. A phrase from the theme tune of *Z Cars* accompanies the police car driving through town and there's a musical tribute to Harry H Corbett's popular TV role, when the clip-clop notes from *Steptoe and Son* follow his horse and cart along the cobbled streets.

Right: Dr Watt (Kenneth Williams) may already be dead – revived by timely doses of electricity to unleash horrific havoc on an unsuspecting world – but he can still be killed when he finds himself 'frying tonight' on the menu in one of his own evil inventions. 'Fangs ain't what they used to be', he regrets as he goes down.

Below: Detective-Sergeant Bung (Harry H Corbett) questions the police surgeon Dr Fettle (Jon Pertwee) about a stray organ they found. 'What's this ear?' he asks. 'It's ear today and gone tomorrow', comes the quick reply in this punning sequence.

Harry H. Corbett	Detective-Sergeant Bung
Kenneth Williams	Dr Watt
Jim Dale	Albert
Charles Hawtrey	Dan Dann
Fenella Fielding	Valeria
Joan Sims	Emily Bung
Angela Douglas	Doris Mann
Bernard Bresslaw	Sockett
Peter Butterworth	Constable Slobotham

Also starred:

Jon Pertwee, Tom Clegg, Frank Thornton, Frank Forsyth, Anthony Sagar and Sally Douglas.

Producer	Peter Rogers
Director	Gerald Thomas
Screenplay	Talbot Rothwell
Music composed and conducted by	Eric Rogers
Song 'Carry on Screaming'	Myles Rudge and Ted Dicks
Cinematographer	Alan Hume RSC
Editor	Rod Keys

97 min. Eastman Color. 1966. Cert. A.

Above: one of Dr Watt's creations, Oddbod (Tom Clegg), is out on the prowl looking for women – but he finds a very fetching Constable Slobotham (Peter Butterworth) instead.

Carry On – Don't Lose Your Head

'Every five minutes a sliced loaf' is the watchword of Citizen Camembert, the big cheese of the French Revolutionary secret police – a proud boast which stirs into action one of English society's most distinguished and fashionable layabouts, Sir Rodney Ffing, henceforth known as The Black Fingernail.

This swashbuckling adventure sees Sid James at his jauntiest as 'that fiddlesome fop' Sir Rodney Ffing, alias The Black Fingernail, who pops up all over Paris rescuing the French aristocracy in the nick of time from the dreaded guillotine. The know-all but see-nothing Chief of the Secret Police, Citizen Camembert (Kenneth Williams), fails to penetrate his numerous disguises – coachman, soldier, insurance agent – even when he appears at the Police office itself as a saucy woman of the night. To add insult to injury, The Black Fingernail's trademark is a note left at the scene of the crime displaying two fingers rampant, one with a blackened nail.

There's a lot of coming and going between England and France. Sir Rodney falls in love with the beautiful Jacqueline (Dany Robin), who helps him escape from the French soldiers before being captured herself. Citizen Camembert and buxom title hunter Desirée Dubarry (Joan Sims) turn up, in the guise of the Duke and Duchess de la Plume de ma Tante, at a dazzling ball at Sir Rodney's elegant country mansion. ('You've always had magnificent balls', says Elspeth March, grandly, in a tiny cameo role as Lady Binder.)

All the familiar ingredients of the English country house drama are woven into action – the stately gavottes in the ballroom, a rendezvous in the arbour of love, a duel at dawn and, finally, a return to France to rescue the beautiful Jacqueline.

At the magnificent chateau which Camembert has presented to himself for services unrendered, Sir Rodney moves into action, aided by his fellow layabout Lord Darcy (Jim Dale) and the Duc de Pommfritt (Charles Hawtrey) who nearly 'had his chips' on the guillotine. The climax is a Fairbanks-and-Flynn style sword-fight, with Sir Rodney and his friends taking on all comers, swinging from chandeliers and sliding down bannisters while the distraught Citizen Camembert tears his hair at the sight of his valuable vases and priceless furniture being shattered.

One of the most elegantly mounted of the series, *Don't Lose Your Head* made use of stately locations at Clandon Park, Waddesdon Manor and Cliveden. It marked a change of distributor from Anglo Amalgamated to Rank.

Opposite: in one of his canny disguises, The Black Fingernail, alias Sir Rodney Ffing (alias Sid James) attempts a daring rescue of a member of the French aristocracy.

Above left: the Duc de Pommfrit (Charles Hawtrey), Sir Rodney Ffing (Sid James) and Lord Darcy (Jim Dale) do their imitation of The Three Musketeers.

Left: Citizen Bidet (Peter Butterworth) has failed his master, Citizen Camembert (Kenneth Williams) yet again as he lets him out of the closet.

Sidney James Sir Rodney Ffing
Kenneth Williams Citizen Camembert
Jim Dale Lord Darcy
Charles Hawtrey Duc de Pommfrit
Joan Sims Desirée Dubarry
Peter Butterworth Citizen Bidet
Dany Robin Jacqueline
Peter Gilmore Robespierre

Also starred:
Marianne Stone, Michael Ward, Leon Greene, David Davenport, Richard Shaw, Jennifer Chulow, Valerie Van Ost and Jacqueline Pearce.

Uncredited:
Elspeth March (Lady Binder), Julian Orchard (Rake) and Billy Cornelius (Soldier).

Producer Peter Rogers
Director Gerald Thomas
Screenplay Talbot Rothwell
Music Eric Rogers

Song
'Don't Lose Your Head' by Bill Martin and Phil Coulter
Sung by the Michael Summers Singers

Cinematographer Alan Hume RSC
Editor Rod Keys

90 min. Eastman Color. 1966. Cert. A

'There's many a fiddle played on an old dune'.

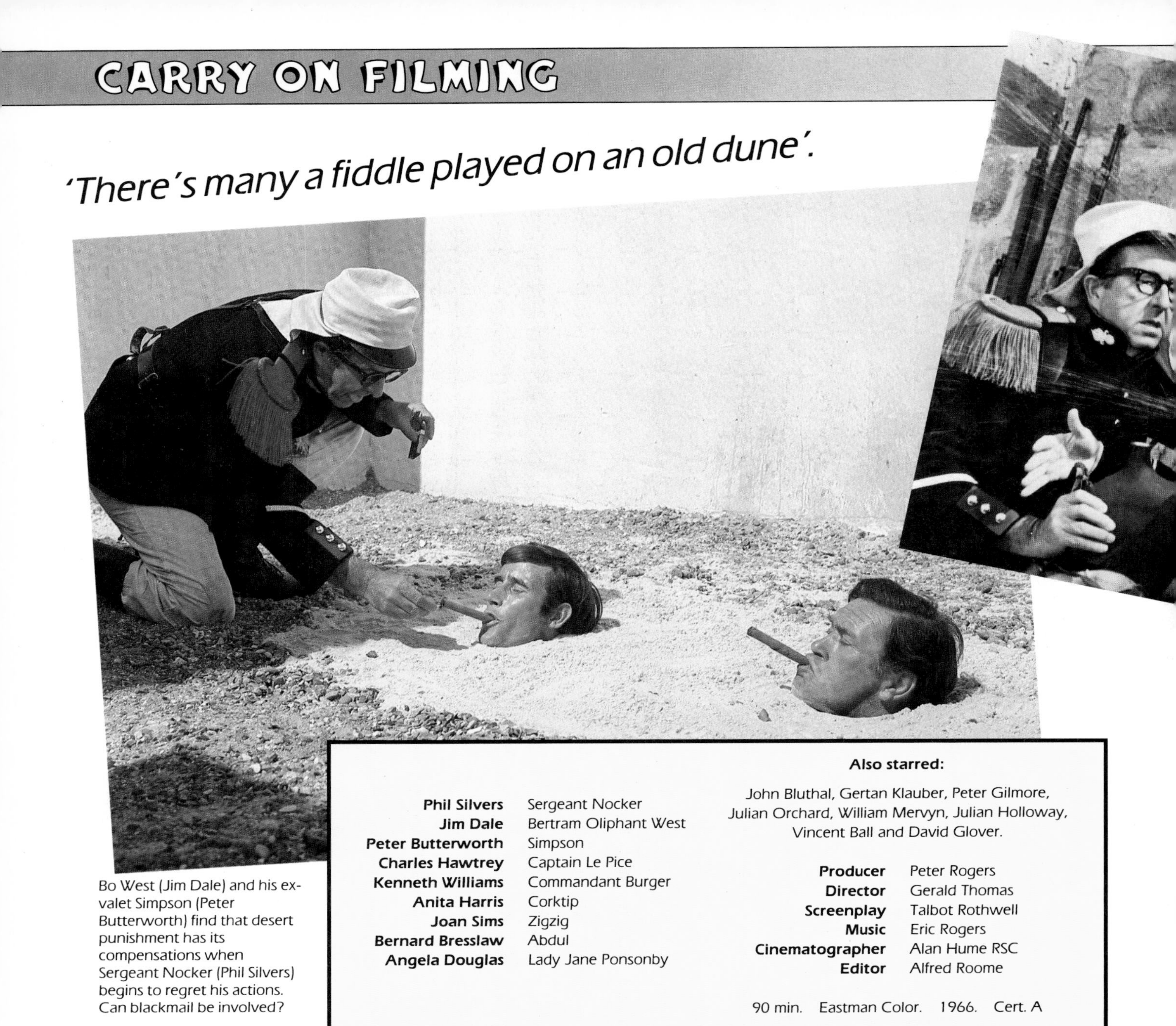

Bo West (Jim Dale) and his ex-valet Simpson (Peter Butterworth) find that desert punishment has its compensations when Sergeant Nocker (Phil Silvers) begins to regret his actions. Can blackmail be involved?

Phil Silvers	Sergeant Nocker
Jim Dale	Bertram Oliphant West
Peter Butterworth	Simpson
Charles Hawtrey	Captain Le Pice
Kenneth Williams	Commandant Burger
Anita Harris	Corktip
Joan Sims	Zigzig
Bernard Bresslaw	Abdul
Angela Douglas	Lady Jane Ponsonby

Also starred:

John Bluthal, Gertan Klauber, Peter Gilmore, Julian Orchard, William Mervyn, Julian Holloway, Vincent Ball and David Glover.

Producer	Peter Rogers
Director	Gerald Thomas
Screenplay	Talbot Rothwell
Music	Eric Rogers
Cinematographer	Alan Hume RSC
Editor	Alfred Roome

90 min. Eastman Color. 1966. Cert. A

Carry On - Follow That Camel

Bertram Oliphant West, known to his friends as Bo West, is accused of conduct unbecoming on the cricket pitch, surrenders his claim to the hand of Lady Jane Ponsonby and, with his faithful manservant in tow, does the gentlemanly thing and joins the Foreign Legion.

The year is 1906. The action begins and ends on the playing fields of England. In between, the desert calls as Bo West tries to clear his unjustly besmirched name. But in typical Carry On style, it is a rather homely desert, with some sad palm trees swaying over a stretch of sand which looks suspiciously like the Sussex Coast. 'There's many a good fiddle played on an old dune', says Commander Burger (Kenneth Williams), the grim Teutonic leader of the Legionnaires in one of his rare moments of frivolity.

American vaudeville artiste Phil Silvers, well-known to TV viewers as Sergeant Bilko, was imported to star in his only British film, a high-spirited satire of the Foreign Legion adventure epics. In a spirited take-off of the all-American hero, he plays the boastful Sergeant Nocker, a compulsive liar who wins medals for self-reported deeds of valour while spending his time in the back room of the Cafe Zigzag with its alluring, hot-tempered proprietress Zigzig (Joan Sims).

The fearsome Riff leader, Abdul Abulbul (Bernard Bresslaw) has a poor opinion of the British. 'It has been truly said', he intones, 'that the mind of the Infidel is like the action of the cleanser – clean round the bend'. He has faith in the great prophet Mustapha Leek, who has decreed that all Legionnaires will die. The Riff custom of falling down in obeisance whenever the name of the prophet is mentioned gives a small advantage to the Legionnaires, once they've learned the trick.

With the aid of a seductive belly-dancer (Anita Harris in the first of her two Carry Ons) Abdul lures the gentlemanly Bo West (Jim Dale), his manservant Simpson (Peter Butterworth) and Sergeant Nocker into captivity on the Oasis El Nookie. During an escape bid they come upon lah-di-dah Lady Jane Ponsonby (Angela Douglas), Bo's ex-fiancée, who has followed him to the desert and has made herself very comfortable – and available – in the harem tent.

The high point of the film is the Legionnaires' march across the desert to reach Fort Zuassantneuf, arriving in time to defend it from an impending attack by the dreaded Riffs. Trekking across the sands under a burning blue sun, one by one the gallant band of Legionnaires succumbs to heat, thirst and tantalizing mirages, while an explanatory map shows that all the time they have been looping a good many loops in their efforts to get from A to B.

As in all good adventure yarns, everything turns out for the best. West gets his woman, Nocker gets his medals, and Abdul Abulbul gets his revenge.

Above: Sheik Abdul Abulbul (Bernard Bresslaw) entertains his guests in style at his desert camp. He is famous for his sayings like 'the behaviour of the white infidel is like blood coming from a stone – a bleeding mystery'. **Top:** Sergeant Nocker and Bo West assist Commandant Burger (Kenneth Williams) after he has been shot.

Carry On Doctor

or Nurse Carries On Again
or Death of a Daffodil
or Life Is a Four-lettered Word

The popular and romantic Dr Kilmore, having been caught in a compromising position on the roof of the nurses' home, gets the sack and the patients – determined to get him reinstated – rise up in rebellion to wreak a frightful revenge on the fierce and formidable Matron and the stubborn, sarcastic Dr Tinkle.

'Oh no you don't', said Mr Bigger as a nurse approaches his bed with a bunch of daffodils. 'Not that! I saw that film.'

In the middle of the successful run of hysterical historicals, the Carry On series returned to the hospital in an attempt to recapture the high spirits – and the best joke – of *Carry On Nurse*. There is also a passing nod to Ralph Thomas' film when a portrait of James Robertson Justice, the fearsome senior surgeon of the Doctor series, is glimpsed in a hospital corridor.

All the Carry On team are there in style: Sidney James smoking under the bedclothes (in reality he was too ill to get out of bed for the filming); Charles Hawtrey suffering a sympathetic pregnancy; Bernard Bresslaw, with his foot encased in plaster, chatting up Dilys Laye; Peter Butterworth with an unexplained lump on his belly; Barbara Windsor popping out of her nurse's uniform; and, of course, Kenneth Williams as the supercilious Dr Tinkle and Hattie Jacques as the Matron. Frankie Howerd makes his first appearance in a Carry On as Mr Bigger, a faith healer. 'What is mind? No matter. What is matter? Never mind', he expounds to a spellbound audience. Joan Sims gives an

Dr Tinkle (Kenneth Williams) finds his blood pressure raised so fast by Matron (Hattie Jacques) that he doesn't mind what he drinks to swallow a quick tranquillizer. The Hattie-Kenneth on/off affair is a regular feature of the hospital Carry Ons.

Frankie Howerd	Francis Bigger
Sidney James	Charlie Roper
Kenneth Williams	Doctor Tinkle
Charles Hawtrey	Mr Barron
Jim Dale	Doctor Kilmore
Barbara Windsor	Sandra May
Joan Sims	Chloe Gibson
Hattie Jacques	Matron
Anita Harris	Nurse Clarke
Bernard Bresslaw	Ken Biddle
Peter Butterworth	Mr Smith

Also starred:

June Jago, Dilys Laye, Derek Francis, Peter Gilmore, Dandy Nichols, Julian Orchard, Julian Holloway, Peter Jones, Deryck Guyler and Gwendoline Watts.

Uncredited:

Pat Coombs (Patient), Penelope Keith (Plain Nurse) and Simon Cain.

Producer	Peter Rogers
Director	Gerald Thomas
Screenplay	Talbot Rothwell
Music	Eric Rogers
Cinematographer	Alan Hume RSC
Editor	Alfred Roome

94 min. Eastman Color. 1968. Cert. A.

Above: the female patients take their revenge on the austere and bossy Matron by giving her the treatment all patients dread – a blanket bath.

Right: romance blossoms in the laboratories as Nurse Clark (Anita Harris) falls for the clumsy but understanding Dr Kilmore (Jim Dale).

untypical performance as his mousy assistant whose deafness is the butt of many a cruel joke.

The finale, as in *Nurse*, is another threatened DIY operation. The rebelling male patients, dressed in surgeons' gowns, strap Dr Tinkle to the operating table, sharpen their scalpels and advance towards his nether regions. The knives don't scare him but, in a boisterous play on everybody's hospital hang-ups, the threat of an enema forces him to yield, while in the women's ward, Matron is defeated by the horrors of a blanket bath.

PRODUCER'S NOTE

My wife, Betty Box, and Gerald's brother, Ralph Thomas, had established a very successful 'Doctor' series with such films as *Doctor in the House*, *Doctor in Clover*, and *Doctor in Trouble*.

When I asked John Davis, head of the Rank Organization, if I could use the title 'Carry On Doctor', John chuckled and said, 'You'd better fix that with your wife'. I did fix it with my wife. I gave her a percentage.

Sidney James	Sir Sidney Ruff-Diamond
Kenneth Williams	The Khazi of Kalabar
Charles Hawtrey	Private James Widdle
Roy Castle	Captain Keene
Joan Sims	Lady Ruff-Diamond
Bernard Bresslaw	Bungdit Din
Peter Butterworth	Missionary
Terry Scott	Sergeant-Major MacNutt
Angela Douglas	Princess Jelhi
Cardew Robinson	The Fakir
Julian Holloway	Major Shorthouse

Also starred:

Peter Gilmore, Leon Thau, Wanda Ventham, Alexandra Dane, Michael Mellinger, Dominique Don, Derek Sydney, Steven Scott and David Spenser.

Uncredited:
Johnny Briggs (Sporran Soldier) and Simon Cain (Bagpipes Soldier).

Producer	Peter Rogers
Director	Gerald Thomas
Screenplay	Talbot Rothwell
Music	Eric Rogers
Cinematographer	Alan Hume RSC
Editor	Alfred Roome

88 min. Eastman Color. 1968. Cert. A.

Above: the Third Foot and Mouth Regiment are ordered to lift their kilts on parade to prove to their commanding officers that unmanly practices – like the wearing of underwear – have not become commonplace.

Right: the intrepid British soldiers (from left to right: Peter Butterworth, Terry Scott, Charles Hawtrey and Roy Castle) enter the harem, in disguise.

Below: Private Widdle (Charles Hawtrey) guards the entrance to the Khyber Pass.

Carry On Up the Khyber

or the British Position in India

The kilted Third Foot and Mouth Regiment let the side down and get caught with their pants up, encouraging the Khazi of Kalabar to attack the garrison while the upper lips of Sir Sidney Ruff-Diamond and his memsahib remain stiffly British.

India has long been a colourful and exotic location for films which demonstrate the moral fibre of the British and their courage on the battlefield. Earnest adventure epics like *The Lives of a Bengal Lancer* (1935) and *Gunga Din* promoted the daring and bravery of the Raj in large screen romantic adventures. When the Carry On team were let loose on the subject, they put their own perspective on it.

The awesome Khyber Pass in this, one of the most satirical films of the series, is a homely five-bar gate (bearing the legend PLEASE SHUT THE GATE) near a ramshackle shed on a rugged patch of hillside in the Snowdonia region of Wales.

The British residency in the nearby town is defended by the Third Foot and Mouth, a gallant regiment of Scots whose fearsome fame as the Devils in Skirts has struck terror into the hearts of the Indian Burpas.

Their reputation for invincibility suffers a rude blow, however, when a rumour is spread that they all wear woolly pants under their kilts. Talbot Rothwell's script milks this old chestnut for all it is worth and the humour is carried to what *The Times'* critic described as 'a new height of happy delirium'. Rothwell's genius for dreaming up appositely absurd names is at its peak, and the film boasts Randy Lal, the Khazi of Kalabar, Bunghit Din, Private Widdle, Sergeant-Major MacNutt and Princess Jelhi.

What a pleasant dish to serve before Sir Sidney Ruff-Diamond (Sid James) and the missionary (Peter Butterworth). The head belongs to the Fakir (Cardew Robinson).

The funniest episode, a classic of the series, is the dinner-party sequence. The Burpas are mounting a full-scale attack on the British residency. Walls are crumbling, windows are blown to smithereens. Inside, the British are dining in style. A uniformed orchestra dodges the falling rubble without missing a note of its Palm Court rendition of a Strauss waltz. Sir Sidney (Sidney James), his memsahib (Joan Sims) and senior army officers serenely savour their meal, apparently oblivious of the thunder of cannon, the collapsing ceiling and the shattering glass.

Slightly the worse for wine, the memsahib brushes some ceiling rubble from her elegant gown. 'Oh dear', she says in her choicest accent, 'I seem to have got a little plastered'.

This, by common consent, is one of the very best Carry Ons – handsomely mounted, briskly paced (thanks to Alfred Roome's deft editing), full of fireworks – and as crude and corny as they come.

PRODUCER'S NOTE

You wouldn't believe that the Rank Organization's 'title consultants' wanted to call this film 'Carry On The Regiment', no doubt fearing some come-back from their 'country-house' fellows who might consider the original title suggestive and out of keeping with the fine traditions of the Rank Organization.

During the making of *Khyber*, I was called back from location to help entertain Princess Margaret who was due to lunch at the studio. In the course of the conversation Princess Margaret asked me, 'Where is your director?' 'He's up Snowdon', I replied.

When the film was shown, I received a letter from an old campaigner who had served in the Khyber Pass during those turbulent times. He said he recognized the place at once!

'The only thing I'm good at, you get struck off for'.

Kenneth Williams	Frederick Carver
Jim Dale	Dr James Nookey
Sidney James	Gladstone Screwer
Joan Sims	Ellen Moore
Charles Hawtrey	Dr Ernest Stoppidge
Barbara Windsor	Goldie Locks
Hattie Jacques	Matron
Patsy Rowlands	Miss Fosdick

Also starred:

Lucy Griffiths, Ann Lancaster, Patricia Hayes, Peter Butterworth, Gwendoline Watts, Peter Gilmore, Pat Coombs, William Mervyn, Billy Cornelius and Elspeth March.

Uncredited:
Wilfred Brambell (Patient) and Shakira Baksh (Scrubba).

Producer	Peter Rogers
Director	Gerald Thomas
Screenplay	Talbot Rothwell
Music	Eric Rogers
Cinematographer	Ernest Steward RSC
Editor	Alfred Roome

89 min. Eastman Color. 1969. Cert. A.

Above: Dr Nookey (Jim Dale) is in trouble again, this time on the consulting room floor with Goldie Locks (Barbara Windsor) to the amusement of Gladstone Screwer (Sid James) and Matron (Hattie Jacques).

Left: Lady Puddleton, alias Dr Ernest Stoppidge alias Charles Hawtrey, becomes unexpectedly bashful when she has to help Mrs Moore (Joan Sims) with her corsets.

Below: Dr Nookey (Jim Dale) bemoans his fate on being posted to the dreadful Beatific Islands and the company of Gladstone Screwer (Sid James).

Carry On Again Doctor

or Where There's a Pill There's A Way
or The Bowels Are Ringing
or If You Say It's Your Thermometer I'll Have To Believe You But It's a Funny Place To Put It

Dr Nookey fails to get any; Gladstone Screwer never stops; Mr Carver can't; Dr Stoppidge won't; and Mrs Moore can't get enough.

Dr Nookey (Jim Dale) disgraces himself at the hospital staff dance ('the only thing I'm good at, you get struck off for') and is exiled to a medical mission on the remote, rain-swamped and mosquito-ridden Beatific Island. Having been given a secret slimming potion by the medical orderly Gladstone Screwer (Sidney James), he flies back to England to make his fortune with a chain of slimming clinics. Everyone wants a piece of the action including Screwer and Nookey's enemies, Mr Carver (Kenneth Williams) and Dr Stoppidge (Charles Hawtrey).

Barbara Windsor, with higher principles but scantier clothing than normal, is Goldie Locks, the dancer who holds out on Nookey for wedding bells. In contrast to his usual Carry On persona, Charles Hawtrey's Dr Stoppidge is severe and forbidding ('I do not object to jiggery but I do take exception to pokery'). But he makes a lovely Lady Puddleton when he gatecrashes the clinic in drag in a bid to steal the formula. Kenneth Williams as head surgeon Frederick Carver is as haughty as ever, insisting that 'I'm a cut above the rest', while Hattie Jacques as Matron and Joan Sims as the wealthy Mrs Moore are kindlier and calmer than they've ever been.

Carry On Camping

or Let Sleeping Bags Lie

Sid and Bernie try to get Joan and Anthea into their sleeping bags; Peter Potter tries to get Charlie Muggins out of his; Matron has her eye on Dr Soper and everybody has theirs on Babs.

'ALL ASSES MUST BE SHOWN' runs the notice by the entrance gate of Paradise Camp Site. This confirms the beliefs of Joan (Joan Sims) and Anthea (Dilys Laye) that they have been brought to a nudist camp site by their frustrated boyfriends, Sid (Sidney James) and Bernie (Bernard Bresslaw), since they have all seen one of the 'nudie' films which were going the rounds in the 60s. Their fears are allayed, and their boyfriends hopes dashed, when it turns out that the owner, Joshua Fiddler (Peter Butterworth), has 'gone for a pee' and returns with the letter P to be tacked onto the notice in the appropriate place.

Also descending on the camp site are a coachload of sexy schoolgirls (with Barbara Windsor's Babs to the fore) determined to get their pernickety headmaster, Dr Soper (Kenneth Williams), into the bed of the passionate school Matron (Hattie Jacques).

In another tent are the hapless, put-upon Peter Potter (Terry Scott) and his domineering 'no sex, please, we're British' wife Harriet played by Betty Marsden with jolly hockey sticks heartiness and an unforgettable braying laugh. They arrive by tandem with Harriet, inevitably, in the driving seat. Meanwhile Charles Hawtrey as the lone hiker, Charlie Muggins, has lost his tent and insists on sleeping between them.

There's a lot of fun with tent-pegs and guy-ropes, a riot of double entendres over poles and fly-sheets, and an epidemic of flirtations, jealousies and misunderstandings. Honours for the best line go to Peter Potter, whose wife never listens to a word of his increasingly wild fantasies. He tells a story of a man camping in Scotland – 'His wife was ravished by a wild haggis And now they're expecting a little faggot'.

Right: Peter and Harriet Potter (Terry Scott and Betty Marsden) have problems when Peter is shot in an uncomfortable position with an air rifle by an irate farmer.

Right: catching cold on the campsite are (from left to right) Bernie (Bernard Bresslaw), Sid (Sid James), Joan (Joan Sims) and Anthea (Dilys Laye) while Joshua Fiddler (Peter Butterworth), the money-grubbing owner looks contentedly on.

Sidney James	Sid Boggle
Charles Hawtrey	Charlie Muggins
Joan Sims	Joan Fussey
Kenneth Williams	Dr Soper
Terry Scott	Peter Potter
Barbara Windsor	Babs
Hattie Jacques	Miss Haggerd
Bernard Bresslaw	Bernie Lugg
Julian Holloway	Jim Tanner
Dilys Laye	Anthea Meeks
Peter Butterworth	Joshua Fiddler
Betty Marsden	Harriet Potter

Also starred:

Trisha Noble, Amelia Bayntum, Patricia Franklin, Derek Francis, Michael Nightingale, Elizabeth Knight, George Moon, Sandra Caron, Valerie Shute, Georgina Moon, Vivien Lloyd, Jennifer Pyle, Lesley Duff, Jackie Poole, Anna Karen, Sally Kemp and Valerie Leon.

Producer	Peter Rogers
Director	Gerald Thomas
Screenplay	Talbot Rothwell
Music	Eric Rogers
Cinematographer	Ernest Steward RSC
Editor	Alfred Roome

88 min. Eastman Color. 1969. Cert. A.

'His wife was ravished by a wild haggis. And now they are expecting a little faggot'.

Camping was shot in icy November weather – no joke for the players, who had to maintain the appearance of happy summer holiday-makers in minimal clothing. Much of the field used for the caravan site was squelching with mud. The art department had to spray it green to sustain the illusion of summer.

Above: no, it's not Bernie and Sid having a night on the tiles. They are, in fact, infiltrating a hippy gathering to try to restore peace and quiet to the campsite.

Left: cheeky Babs (Barbara Windsor) finds – to the onlookers' delight – that she cannot contain herself during the morning's physical education exercises.

In the climatic action scene the campers, enraged by the noise from a hippy rave-up in the next field, mount a well-planned operation which sends them on their way, taking the schoolgirls with them in a joyful procession.

PRODUCER'S NOTE

This film was shot in the depths of our English spring, in freezing temperatures and with the fields deep in mud. Snow fell during the shooting but the cameraman, Ernest Stewart, carried on declaring, 'We'll pretend it's blossom.'

It was in this film that the mud was sprayed with green paint. Barbara Windsor, with a live throat mike, trudged through it cursing me and calling me all the names she could think of – and her vocabulary in that respect was prodigious. When during the 'rushes' I heard the oaths directed at me, I decided to leave them for the later running, when the artistes and technicians see their rushes. Barbara was horrified and not a little frightened, quite convinced that she would be fired when the producer saw the rushes. When she was told that I had already seen them and had approved, she realized that she was being 'had.'

Carry On Up The Jungle

or the African Queen
or Stop Beating About the Bush
or Show Me Your Waterhole and I'll Show You Mine

Lady Evelyn Bagley joins an expedition to darkest Africa to seek her long-lost baby; Professor Inigo Tinkle and his assistant Claude Chumley are seeking the legendary Oozalum bird; and fearless white hunter Bill Boosey is seeking anything in a skirt.

For 50 years, Tarzan had been cinema's King of The Jungle, happily oblivious to the fate which lay in store for him when he fell into the anarchic hands of the Carry On team.

Made in darkest Pinewood, *Carry On Up The Jungle* contains some token wild-life stock footage. But, true to type, its star animal is a fancy-dress gorilla which, like Sid James' Bill Boosey, has a lecherous, roving eye.

Terry Scott is the plump and babyfaced Jungle Boy, swinging from mangy ropes, crashlanding on rotting branches and disastrously ignoring the warning sign DANGER – CONCEALED TREE. Jacki Piper, maid-servant to Lady Evelyn, is his dewy-eyed but far from innocent Jane.

Frankie Howerd, playing the ornithologist Inigo Tinkle in the second of his two Carry Ons, fills the puritanical egghead role usually reserved for Kenneth Williams. His conversation oozes with earnest erudition. Told about a snake that rocks its head rigidly from side to side, he promptly identifies it as a harmless Vindscreen Viper. Asked why giraffes have such long necks, he is ready with the explanation, 'Oh, it's quite simple', he says in his most professorial tone, 'It's because their heads are so far from their bodies'.

'One would feel so much safer with a strong, fearless man beside one,' says Lady Evelyn (Joan Sims doing her imperious bit to perfection) in a non-too-subtle attempt to lure the Professor into her tent as the evening falls. 'Oh, I agree,' says the Prof 'but where could we find one out here?'

Bedroom farce takes on a new meaning when the sleeping-quarters are a circle of lamplit tents, the only loos are the jungle bushes and the bed-swappers include the primitive Jungle Boy and the randy gorilla.

Marauding animals, hostile tribesmen, and cannibals

Left: even a randy gorilla has difficulty with his/her reading.
Below: the Carry On safari to darkest Africa hits rock bottom when they are captured by the all-girl tribe, the Lubby-Dubbys from Afrodisia.

Frankie Howerd	Professor Inigo Tinkle
Sidney James	Bill Boosey
Charles Hawtrey	Tonka
Joan Sims	Lady Evelyn Bagley
Terry Scott	Jungle Boy
Kenneth Connor	Claude Chumley
Bernard Bresslaw	Upsidasi
Jacki Piper	June

Also starred:
Reuben Martin, Valerie Leon, Edwina Carroll, Valerie Moore, Cathi March, Danny Daniels and Yemi Ajibadi.

Uncredited:
Nina Baden-Semper

Producer	Peter Rogers
Director	Gerald Thomas
Screenplay	Talbot Rothwell
Music	Eric Rogers
Cinematographer	Ernest Steward RSC
Editor	Alfred Roome

89 min. Eastman Color. 1970. Cert. A.

stoking the fire beneath a steaming cauldron, are just a few of the familiar screen hazards which the brave explorers have to face – not to mention the giant piles of detritus left whenever there is an elephant charge, which provide the film's crappiest running joke.

The story meanders mazily towards a happy ending. Bill Boosey gets more than enough of what he fancies when the expedition is captured by a female tribe from Aphrodisia, led by the unlikely figure of Charles Hawtrey as the Great Tonka. Lady Evelyn, recognizing the nappy pin which keeps Jungle Boy's homespun jockstrap in place, is able to claim him as her long-lost baby. And who should the Great Tonka turn out to be but her equally long-lost, formerly put-upon husband, Walter?

Professor Tinkle and his sidekick Claude Chumley (Kenneth Connor) find the Oozalum bird and bring it back to England. Highlight of their public lecture is to be the unveiling of the cage containing the rare and celebrated bird. The audience gasps as the Professor pulls off the covering. But the bird has performed its own unique and legendary trick. 'Where's it disappeared to?' he asks, staring into the empty cage in disbelief.

Below: Tarzan (Terry Scott) looks even more like an overgrown baby in nappies when he is being taught to read by the ever-loving June (Jacki Piper). Remember the two different pronunciations of the word 'lead' and you'll realize why Tarzan is grinning at reading the word 'bead'.

Opposite: Professor Tinkle (Frankie Howerd) and Bill Boosey (Sid James) discover that captivity in the hands of the Lubby-Dubbys may not be all bad if their Leda (Valerie Leon) is anything to go by.

Below: the path of true love for Bertie (Richard O'Callaghan) and Sally (Jacki Piper) may be smooth but Jenny (Imogen Hassall) and Terence (Terry Scott) are having trouble.

Above: Sidney Bliss (Sid James) gets his own back on Sophie (Hattie Jacques) at their wedding.

Sidney James	Sidney Bliss
Kenneth Williams	Percival Snooper
Charles Hawtrey	James Bedsop
Joan Sims	Esme Crowfoot
Hattie Jacques	Sophie
Terry Scott	Terence Philpot
Richard O'Callaghan	Bertie Muffet
Bernard Bresslaw	Gripper Burke
Jacki Piper	Sally Martin
Imogen Hassall	Jenny Grubb
Patsy Rowlands	Miss Dempsey

Also starred:

Julian Holloway, Joan Hickson, Bill Maynard, Amelia Bayntum, Tom Clegg, Anthony Sagar, Bill Pertwee, Lauri Lupino Lane and Kenny Lynch.

Uncredited:

Peter Butterworth – guest appearance

Producer	Peter Rogers
Director	Gerald Thomas
Screenplay	Talbot Rothwell
Music	Eric Rogers
Cinematographer	Ernes Steward RSC
Editor	Alfred Roome

88 min. Eastman Color. 1970. Cert. A.

Carry On Loving

Lonelyhearts of Much-Snoggin-in-the-Green come to the Wedded Bliss computer dating agency for potential partners and turn for advice to Sidney Bliss' helpful pamphlet, The Wit to Woo.

Like *Carry On Regardless*, *Carry On Loving* is a series of comic episodes with a common linking theme. At the heart of the film is the Wedded Bliss marriage bureau run by Sidney Bliss (Sidney James). His partner and would-be wife, Sophie (Hattie Jacques), has to use all her skills to restrain him from dating their most attractive customer, the buxom, flighty Esme Crowfoot (Joan Sims).

Sophie's ploy to make Sid jealous by dating Percival Snooper (Kenneth Williams), a marriage guidance counsellor in need of marriage guidance, comes to an abrupt end when his housekeeper (Patsy Rowlands) declares her undying love for him.

Sid's escapades with Esme come to an even quicker end with the arrival of her one-time boyfriend, Gripper Burke (Bernard Bresslaw), a giant wrestler in possessive mood.

Among those searching for Wedded Bliss are bashful Bertie Muffet (Richard O'Callaghan) and photographic model Sally Martin (Jacki Piper); Terence Philpot (Terry Scott) and Jenny Grubb (Imogen Hassall), who is transformed from a plain Jane into a busty beauty.

Carry On Loving is the definitive 'It' film, with the 'It' jokes coming thick and fast. 'Have you had it?' (my blue jumper); 'Let's go straight to my place and do it' (take my photograph); 'I always fancy it in the mornings' (a cup of tea). Even the phonebox, occupied by a loving couple oblivious to callers, joins the club. PLEASE BE QUICK, runs the display notice, OTHERS MAY BE WAITING FOR IT.

Carry On Henry

or Mind My Chopper

Rough King Hal gains two extra wives in a revised version of English history based solely on research by William Cobbler – a preface title note confirms that this version is definitely all Cobbler's.

First there was Charles Laughton in Alexander Korda's *The Private Life of Henry VIII* (1933), a landmark in British cinema. Much later there was Robert Shaw in *A Man for All Seasons* (1966) and Richard Burton (starring opposite Genevieve Bujold) in *Anne of the Thousand Days* (1969). And then there was Sidney James who in 1971 ascended the wellworn throne, donned the mantle of the much-married king – and put his boot through all that pomp.

A gravel-voiced, gorblimey Henry, he is eager to bed his new wife, Marie of Normandy (Joan Sims), but is repelled by her predilection for garlic. She refuses to give it up. He denies her her marital rights. 'Give in to her?', he raves to his courtiers. 'Not on your Nellie'. And he warns her: 'Just don't bother to make any more hairdressing appointments'.

His problem is how to dispose of his malodorous wife without provoking a war with her cousin, the King of France (Peter Gilmore). But while Henry is finding solace in the arms of the pert and wide-eyed Bettina (Barbara Windsor who whispers coyly 'I promised my mother I'd be a good Bett'), Marie is being consoled by the ever-eager Sir Roger de Lodgerly (Charles Hawtrey) and is expecting an heir. In plot and counterplot, with Mr Fawkes, well before his time, ever ready with the gunpowder, the frail Sir Roger is tortured on the rack first for confession, then retraction and then for retraction of retraction – and ends up ten feet tall. 'We'll go to any lengths to get what we want', boasts the scheming Thomas Cromwell (Kenneth Williams).

Joan Sims as Marie, imperiously demanding her rights, gives a deliciously wicked send-up of Genevieve Bujold and the whole film is a preposterous take-off of the solemn *Anne of the Thousand Days*, full of cheeky reminders of Alexander Korda's rumbustious epic.

It is elegantly mounted and costumed with a nice line in sartorial satire provided by the bedraggled dyed boas draped round the floppy Tudor hats of the richly clad men from the courts and castles.

Right: Thomas Cromwell (Kenneth Williams) and Cardinal Wolsey (Terry Scott) would rather face the block than another chaotic term of office with King Henry.
Below: King Henry (Sid James) tucks into a traditional roast watched with amusement by his French, garlic-gobbling Queen (Joan Sims).

'Drink inflames the ardour. The more you drink the harder it gets'.

Sidney James	Henry VIII
Kenneth Williams	Thomas Cromwell
Charles Hawtrey	Sir Roger de Lodgerley
Joan Sims	Queen Marie
Terry Scott	Cardinal Wolsey
Barbara Windsor	Bettina
Kenneth Connor	Lord Hampton of Wick

Also starred:

Julian Holloway, Peter Gilmore, Julian Orchard, Gertan Klauber, Margaret Nolan, Bill Maynard, Dave Prowse, Patsy Rowlands, Billy Cornelius, Leon Green, John Bluthal, Anthony Sagar and Peter Butterworth (guest appearance).

Producer	Peter Rogers
Director	Gerald Thomas
Screenplay	Talbot Rothwell
Music	Eric Rogers
Cinematographer	Alan Hume RSC
Editor	Alfred Roome

89 min. Eastman Color. 1971. Cert. A.

Carry On At Your Convenience

or Down the Spout
or Ladies Please be Seated
or Up the Workers
or Labour Relations Are the People Who Come To See You When You're Having a Baby

Vic Spanner is the 'miserable little leader' of NUCIE, the National Union of Chinaware Industrial Employees at WC Boggs, makers of fine toilet ware, who calls the workers out on any and every technicality and is a regular spanner in the works.

Amid the plethora of lavatory and bidet jokes, there are several amusing sketches, the best of which involves a budgie that chirps out racing tips to Sid Plummer (Sid James) and his wife (Hattie Jacques) who spoil their pet 'to budgery'.

Two things stand out from the rest. One is a neat send-up of the so-called sex education films that were creeping around the seamier cinemas of the period. The other is a gutsy performance from Renee Houston as Vic Spanner's no-nonsense mother.

Left: Agatha Spanner (Renee Houston) resolves the industrial dispute at WC Boggs and Son, which has been sparked off by her bolshie son Vic (Kenneth Cope), in a domestic if rather public way. The workers including Bernie (Bernard Bresslaw), Chloe (Joan Sims) and Beattie (Hattie Jacques) watch with delight.

Below: management, in the shape of WC Boggs (Kenneth Williams), and workers Sid Plummer (Sid James) and Miss Withering (Patsy Rowlands) enjoy a rest from industrial strife on the works outing.

Sidney James	Sid Plummer
Kenneth Williams	WC Boggs
Charles Hawtrey	Charles Coote
Joan Sims	Chloe Moore
Hattie Jacques	Beattie Plummer
Bernard Bresslaw	Bernie Hulke
Kenneth Cope	Vic Spanner
Patsy Rowlands	Miss Withering
Jacki Piper	Myrtle Plummer
Richard O'Callaghan	Lewis Boggs

Also starred:

Bill Maynard, Davy Kaye, Renee Houston, Marianne Stone, Margaret Nolan, Geoffrey Hughes, Hugh Futcher, Simon Cain, Leon Greene and Harry Towb.

Producer	Peter Rogers
Director	Gerald Thomas
Screenplay	Talbot Rothwell
Music	Eric Rogers
Cinematographer	Ernest Steward RSC
Editor	Alfred Roome

90 min. Eastman Color. 1971. Cert. A.

With the help of the local liqueur (a veritable love potion), everyone is coupling off even though the hotel is falling down around their feet.

Sidney James	Vic Flange
Kenneth Williams	Stuart Farquhar
Charles Hawtrey	Eustace Tuttle
Joan Sims	Cora Flange
Bernard Bresslaw	Brother Bernard
Barbara Windsor	Sadie
Kenneth Connor	Stanley Blunt
Peter Butterworth	Pepe
Jimmy Logan	Bert Conway
June Whitfield	Evelyn Blunt
Hattie Jacques	Floella

Also starred:

Derek Francis, Sally Geeson, Ray Brooks, Amelia Bayntum, Carol Hawkins, Gertan Klauber, Jack Douglas, Patsy Rowlands, David Kernan and Bill Maynard.

Producer	Peter Rogers
Director	Gerald Thomas
Screenplay	Talbot Rothwell
Music	Eric Rogers
Cinematographer	Alan Hume RSC
Editor	Alfred Roome

88 min. Eastman Color. 1972. Cert. A.

Carry On Abroad

or What a Package
or It's All In
or Swiss Hols in the Snow

Vic and Cora Flange join a motley assortment of holidaymakers for a four-day package to the Spanish resort of Elsbels and discover the pitfalls – and the pratfalls – of foreign travel.

When the Carry On series began in 1958, Butlins and Blackpool were the favourite comic butts of British holidaymakers. Fourteen years on it was Viva l'Espana and the Mediterranean sun. A new world of leaky loos, rickety balconies and early morning bulldozers had opened out for the great British public.

In *Carry On Abroad*, half of the Elsbels Palace Hotel is still under construction, and the finished half is faultier than Fawlty Towers. Within minutes of the tourists' arrival, the room service line is buzzing with complaints: 'There's a strange man in my bath'; 'My wardrobe's got no back'; 'My drawers have got no bottom'. As Vic (Sidney James) puts it, the hotel has 'more teething troubles than a crocodile with pyorrhoea'.

Little do they know that Pepe – (Peter Butterworth) who is manager, porter, receptionist and telephone operator – has fixed the switchboard so that all the visitors are yelling at each other.

As the days pass, flirtations are rife, tempers flare, husbands and lovers are at each other's throats and, what's worse, it's raining. After a fracas at the local brothel, everyone is carted off to jail.

On the last evening, the farewell party looks more like a wake than a gala – until the tourists sample the punch. It has been secretly laced with Liquora Amorosa, which sends everybody into an amorous spin. Jimmy Logan finally finds Barbara Windsor; Kenneth Connor and June Whitfield end the frustrating years of their marriage; Sidney James resigns himself to his wife, Joan Sims; even Brother Bernard (Bernard Bresslaw) finds his true vocation with Sally Geeson. Everybody, that is, except the hapless Pepe and his kitchen-bound wife Floella (an unexpectedly exotic role for Hattie Jacques) who are the only people to notice that the flood water is pouring in and the entire hotel is collapsing around their ears.

After *Carry On Abroad*, Charles Hawtrey, who plays Eustace Tuttle, a maverick tourist on the razzle, carried on no more.

The ubiquitous Pepe (Peter Butterworth) finds trouble everywhere, even in his kitchen. Floella (Hattie Jacques) is obviously out to cook his bacon.

Sidney James	Sid Carter
Kenneth Williams	Sir Bernard Cutting
Charles Hawtrey	Dr Francis Goode
Joan Sims	Mrs Tidey
Hattie Jacques	Matron
Bernard Bresslaw	Ernie
Kenneth Cope	Cyril Carter
Terry Scott	Dr Prodd
Barbara Windsor	Nurse Susan Ball
Kenneth Connor	Mr Tidey
Jacki Piper	Sister

Also starred:

Bill Maynard, Patsy Rowlands, Derek Francis, Amelia Bayntum, Valerie Leon, Brian Osborne, Gwendoline Watts, Margaret Nolan, Wendy Richard, Bill Kenwright and Jack Douglas.

Uncredited:
Marianne Stone

Producer	Peter Rogers
Director	Gerald Thomas
Screenplay	Talbot Rothwell
Music	Eric Rogers
Cinematographer	Ernest Steward RSC
Editor	Alfred Roome

87 min. Eastman Color. 1972. Cert. A.

Above: surprisingly Dr Cutting (Kenneth Williams) pleads with Matron (Hattie Jacques) – usually it is Matron who does the cajoling.

Right: Sid Carter (Sid James) is always the gentleman – even when surprising girls in the bath.

Carry On Matron

or From Here to Maternity
or Familiarity Breeds
or Womb at the Top
or The Pregger's Opera

A gang of smalltime petty thieving pill-pinchers infiltrate the Finisham Maternity Hospital in a bid to steal the plans and locate the loot, but find it easier to get into the building than out of it.

The 23rd in the series, and the fourth with a hospital background, this one focuses on the doctors at the Maternity Hospital and the pill-thieves who are planning to rob it.

The medics provide the raunchiest source of mirth. Kenneth Williams is at his pottiest as the hypochondriac consultant Sir Bernard Cutting, whose latest neurosis is a fear that he is undergoing a sex-change. Charles Hawtrey is the genial psychiatrist Dr Goode who advises him to prove his manhood in the time-honoured manner. Hattie Jacques, playing her fifth Carry On matron, has to bear the brunt of his self-cure enthusiasms.

Terry Scott, as Dr Prodd, spends so much of his time chasing the nurses that he's known in the wards as the taxidermist.

The pill thieves are led by Sid James as Sid Carter, with Kenneth Cope as his wayward son Cyril and Bernard Bresslaw as his dense henchman Ernie. Cyril cases the joint disguised as a nurse but gets drawn into the hospital routine, Dr Prodd's philanderings and a true love affair with Nurse Ball (Barbara Windsor). Ernie follows by infiltrating the hospital as a mother-to-be, in voluminous maternity dress. On the way in his 'bump' is a bagful of dynamite and fuses. On the way out his 'baby' is a blanket stuffed with the loot.

The only genuinely expectant mum, Mrs Tidy (Joan Sims), whose baby is very much overdue, provides the best running joke by stuffing herself with food throughout the film, raising a series of false alarms which turn out to be indigestion, while her railwayman husband (Kenneth Connor) has kittens in the waiting room. Making a briefer appearance in the waiting room is Jack Douglas in the first of his seven Carry On roles. A nervous expectant father, he returns from the delivery room twitching in every limb. He picks up the phone and utters his single, but memorable, line: 'Get me the Guinness Book of Records'.

Sid Carter's pill-stealing gang are all in disguise when trying to penetrate the Finisham Maternity Hospital. Sid (Sid James) sprouts a beard and glasses; Ernie (Bernard Bresslaw) looks convincing as a new Mum while Cyril (Kenneth Cope) makes a fetching nurse.

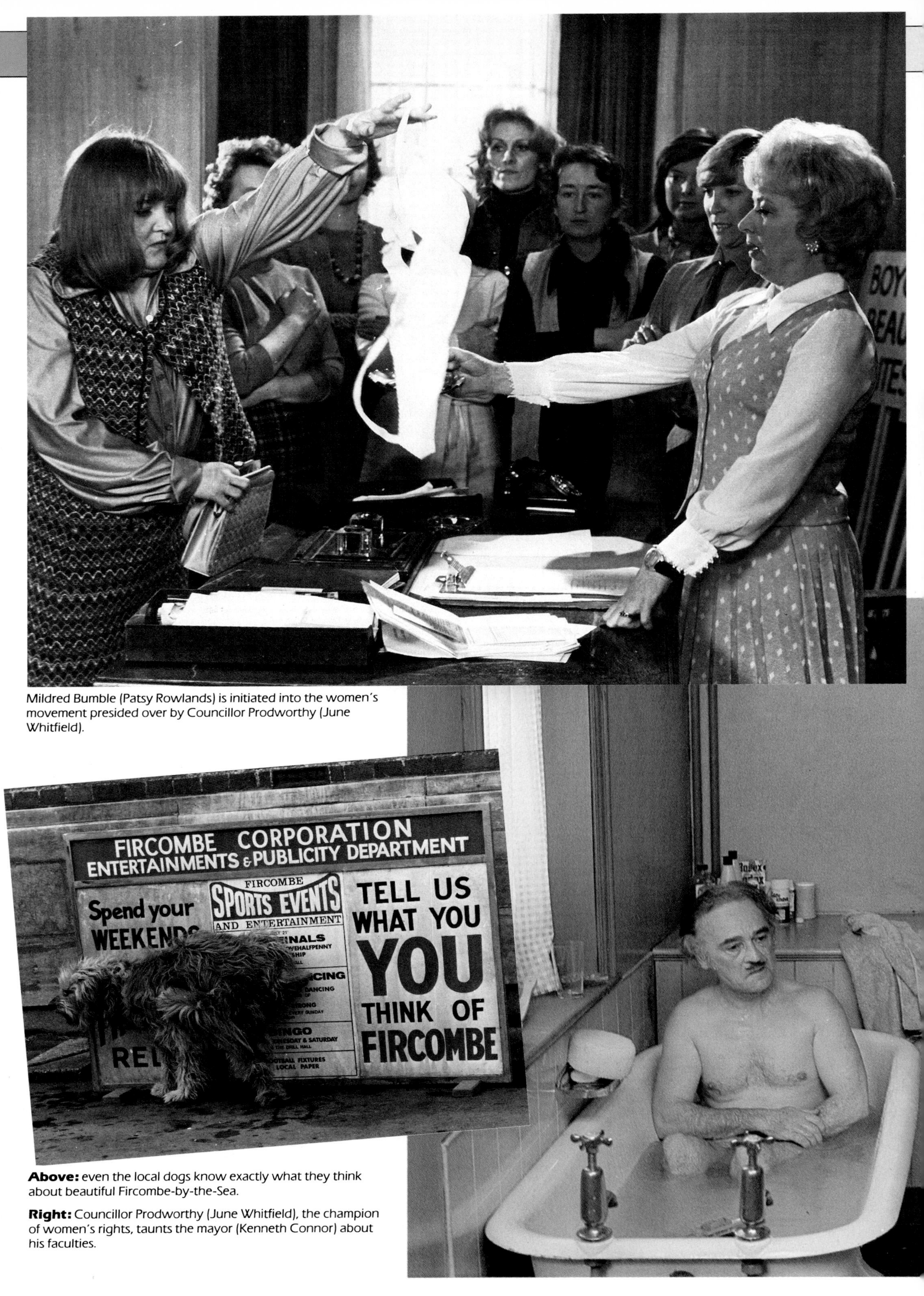

Mildred Bumble (Patsy Rowlands) is initiated into the women's movement presided over by Councillor Prodworthy (June Whitfield).

Above: even the local dogs know exactly what they think about beautiful Fircombe-by-the-Sea.

Right: Councillor Prodworthy (June Whitfield), the champion of women's rights, taunts the mayor (Kenneth Connor) about his faculties.

Carry On Girls

Sidney Fiddler, having persuaded the Mayor of a rundown seaside town to let him pep up its image by staging a beauty contest, comes up against the formidable Councillor Mrs Augusta Prodworthy and her doughty band of Women's Lib saboteurs.

Surprisingly, it took the Carry Ons 25 films to rustle up a beauty contest. They made up for lost time, pitting the wits of Sidney Fiddler (Sidney James) against the might of the Women's Liberation Movement.

June Whitfield, as Augusta Prodworthy, looks more like a stray from the Festival of Light than a typical Women's Libber but she has a splendid line in put-downs. Gazing contemptuously at the ineffectual little Mayor (Kenneth Connor) playing with plastic ducks in his bath, she tells him 'You are as poorly equipped to carry out your civic duties as you are your domestic ones.'

Sidney collects a bevy of Carry On beauties: Barbara Windsor as the clever, gutsy, motorbiking contestant Hope Springs, with Easy Rider studded on her back; Wendy Richard as Ida Downs from Bristol; Margaret Nolan as Dawn Brakes, the former Miss Dairy Queen; Sally Geeson as Deborah; Angela Grant as Miss Bangor; and last, but never least, Bernard Bresslaw in drag.

Final honours go to the Women's Libbers who, joined by the Mayor's long-suffering wife (one of Patsy Rowland's best roles) annihilate the contest with itching powder, sneezing powder, soot bombs and water-sprinklers in a knockabout finale in the best Carry On tradition.

Peter (Bernard Bresslaw) takes to drag when he is persuaded, against his better judgement, to become one of the beauty contestants.

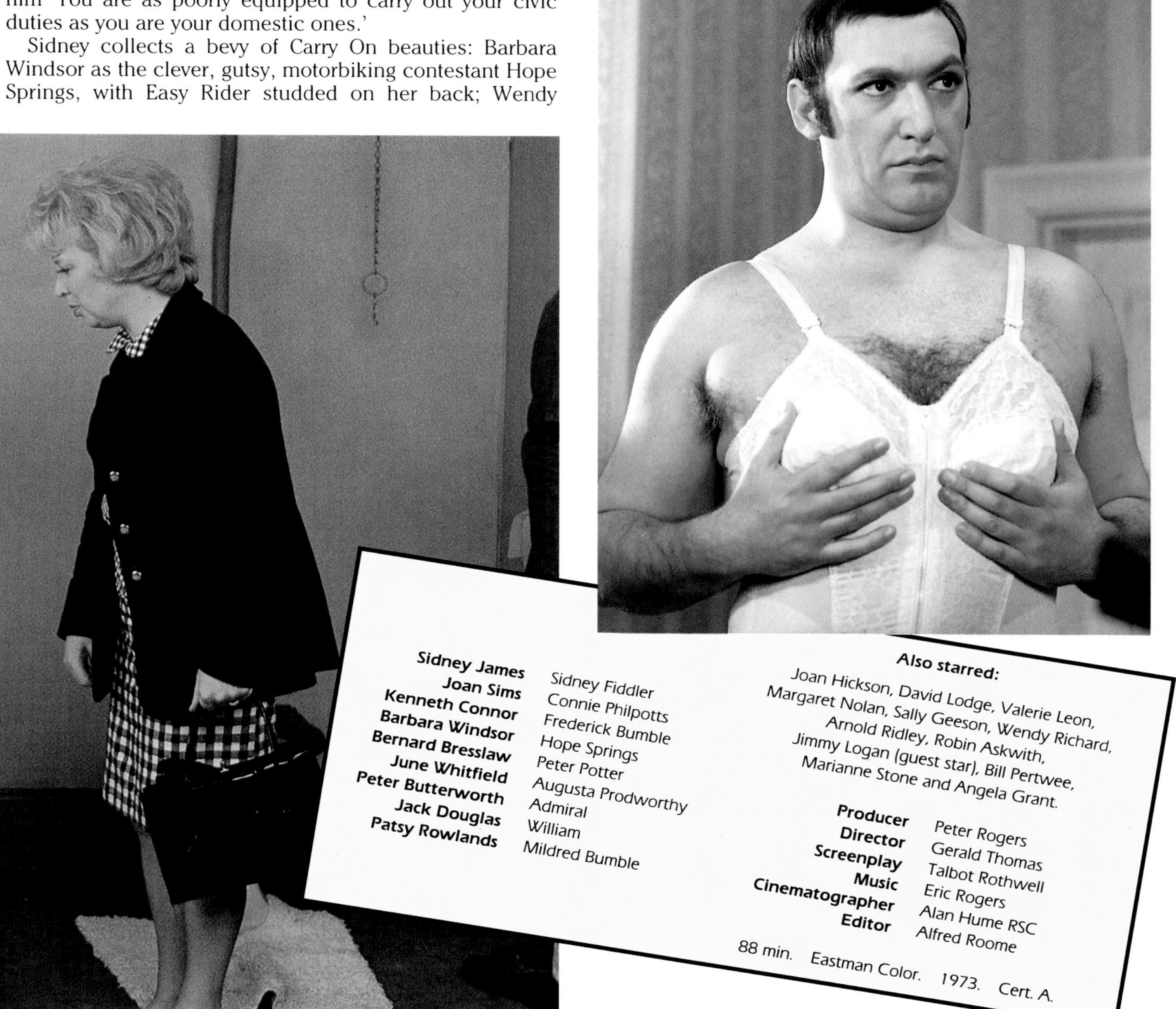

Sidney James	Sidney Fiddler
Joan Sims	Connie Philpotts
Kenneth Connor	Frederick Bumble
Barbara Windsor	Hope Springs
Bernard Bresslaw	Peter Potter
June Whitfield	Augusta Prodworthy
Peter Butterworth	Admiral
Jack Douglas	William
Patsy Rowlands	Mildred Bumble

Also starred:
Joan Hickson, David Lodge, Valerie Leon, Margaret Nolan, Sally Geeson, Wendy Richard, Arnold Ridley, Robin Askwith, Jimmy Logan (guest star), Bill Pertwee, Marianne Stone and Angela Grant.

Producer	Peter Rogers
Director	Gerald Thomas
Screenplay	Talbot Rothwell
Music	Eric Rogers
Cinematographer	Alan Hume RSC
Editor	Alfred Roome

88 min. Eastman Color. 1973. Cert. A.

Carry On Dick

Captain Fancey and Sergeant Jock Strapp of the Bow Street Runners solicit the aid of the Reverend Flasher, rector of the God-fearing village of Upper Dencher, in their hunt for the elusive Dick Turpin, unaware that the Reverend and Big Dick are one and the same man.

At the beginning of the film the voice-over commentary declares: ' "Turpin" was known as Big Dick owing to the size of his weapon. What's more, there is a birthmark on the weapon in question which is the only known positive means of identifying the owner.'

The dialogue is riper than ever, but visually this is a colourful, rip-roaring Carry On, casting a backward glance at the old 'stand and deliver' and 'meet me by the blasted oak' adventure films. Madame Desirée (Joan Sims with a plummy French accent) and her Birds of Paradise arrive by stagecoach to present living tableaux at the old Cock Inn, hijacking a saloon-bar staple of the Western.

Sid James does a dirty double as the Reverend Flasher, the highly respected Vicar who leads a secret life as the elusive Dick Turpin. The Reverend's ears prick up when he hears of the hundred guineas reward for his own capture. 'I would like to get my organ into use again', he says solemnly, without batting an eyelid.

Jack Douglas, who had joined the series in *Carry On Matron*, comes into his own in his fourth Carry On film as Jock Strapp, the twitchy Sergeant of the Bow Street Runners, whose bumbling incompetence ruins the best-laid plans of his superior, the obsequious Captain Fancey (Kenneth Williams).

Men in drag are a familiar feature of Carry Ons. *Carry On Dick* has the Reverend and his verger (Peter Butterworth) gatecrashing the village constabulary disguised as local dames; it also boasts a principal boy in the busty shape of Barbara Windsor's Harry, Turpin's pistol-packing side-kick, more recognizable as Harriet, the Reverend's devoted serving-wench.

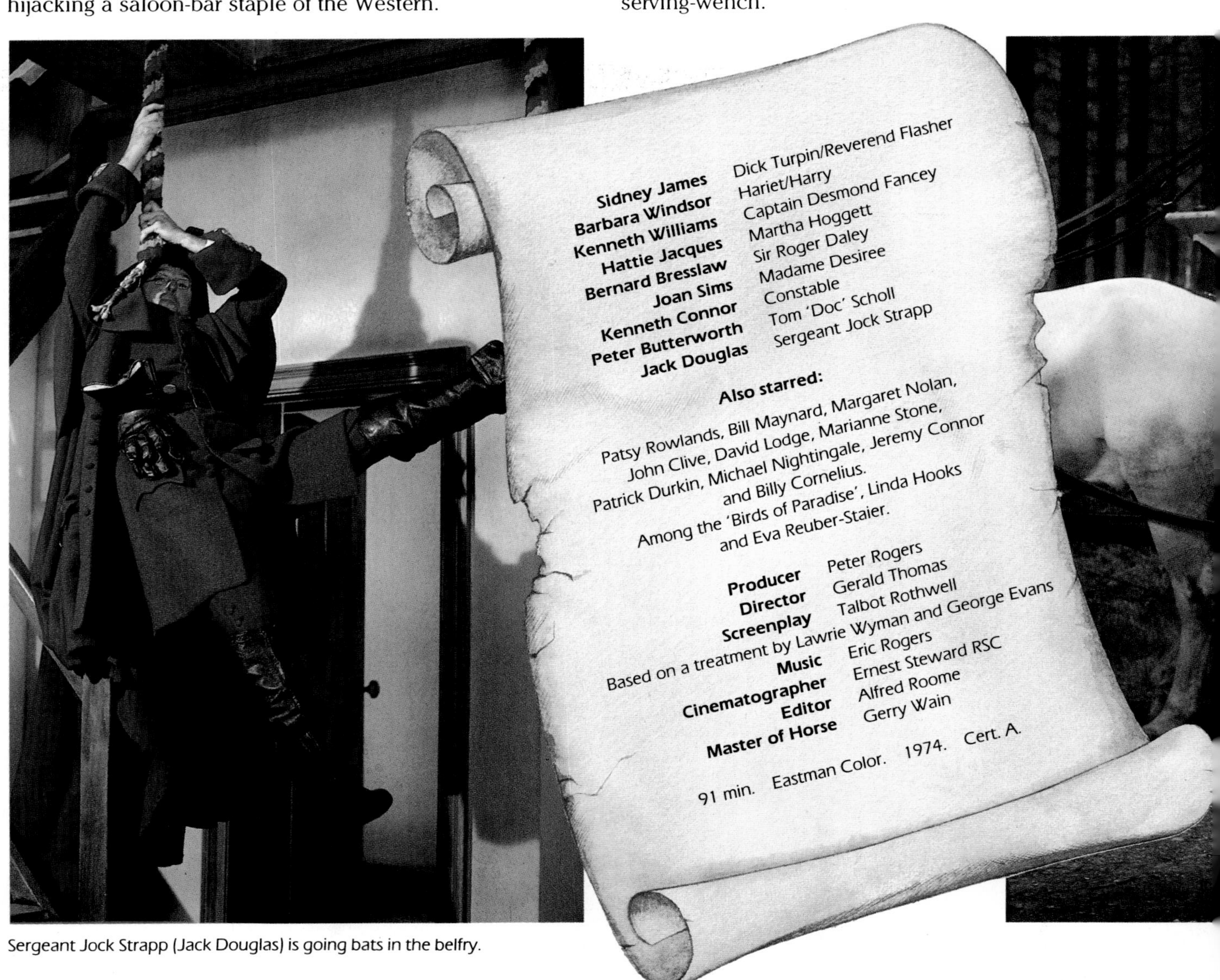

Sergeant Jock Strapp (Jack Douglas) is going bats in the belfry.

Among the most successful of the series, *Carry On Dick* marked the end of a Carry On era. Sadly, it was to be the last of the series for Sid James, who died in 1976 and for Hattie Jacques, cast as the Reverend's faithful housekeeper and organist, who died in 1981.

Above: Sir Roger Daley (Bernard Bresslaw) is left in an altogether embarrassing position when he is robbed by highwayman Dick Turpin.

Above left: from behind the blasted oak, Dick Turpin (Sid James) appears, ready for action on the highway.

'Pistol?' ... 'Haven't had a drop'.

Madame Desirée (Joan Sims) and her Birds of Paradise, who provide the nightly entertainment at the Old Cock Inn, are robbed on the public highway.

Carry On Behind

Major Leep, owner of a run-down caravan site perched on top of an ancient Roman encampment, finds that mixing relic-seeking archaeologists and fun-loving holiday-makers is the perfect recipe for a week of shambolic chaos.

Nearly ten years after *Carry On Camping*, the team returned to the same location for another spree of fresh air and fun. But by this stage of the Carry On game many of the regulars were absent. An injection of fresh talent was needed and international actress Elke Sommer heads the cast. As a Russian archaeologist wrestling bizarrely with the English language she gives a whole new slant to the series' customary double entendres and makes an ideal foil for Kenneth Williams' straight-laced and pompous Professor Crump.

Among the caravaners are Windsor Davies and Jack Douglas, the latter by now a Carry On regular. They are ostensibly on a fishing trip, but amid a plethora of jokes about 'tackle' and 'bait' it soon becomes apparent that they are angling for a different kind of catch.

In another caravan, Patsy Rowlands keeps her eye on her roving husband (Bernard Bresslaw) and her patience with her interfering mother-in-law (Joan Sims). The family's foulmouthed Mynah bird sparks off a chain of misunderstandings.

Dave Freeman replaced Talbot Rothwell as scriptwriter. His scenario is long on incident with running gags involving a giant dog on the rampage and seats which are still wet from a new coat of paint.

Behinds are also bared at the drop of a trouser or skirt and there's a startling full posterior nude shot of Kenneth Williams – a first for the Carry Ons.

Elke Sommer	Professor Anna Vrooshka
Kenneth Williams	Professor Roland Crump
Bernard Bresslaw	Arthur Upmore
Kenneth Connor	Major Leep
Jack Douglas	Ernie Bragg
Joan Sims	Daphne Barnes
Windsor Davies	Fred Ramsden
Peter Butterworth	Barnes
Liz Fraser	Sylvia Ramsden
Patsy Rowlands	Linda Upmore

Also starred:

Ian Lavender, Adrienne Posta, Patricia Franklin, Donald Hewlett, Carol Hawkins, Sherrie Hewson, David Lodge, Marianne Stone, George Layton, Brian Osborne, Larry Dann, Linda Hooks, Billy Cornelius and Jeremy Connor.

Uncredited:
Johnny Briggs and Lucy Griffiths.

Producer	Peter Rogers
Director	Gerald Thomas
Screenplay	Dave Freeman
Music	Eric Rogers
Cinematographer	Ernest Steward RSC
Editor	Alfred Roome

90 min. Eastman Color. 1975. Cert. A.

Opposite: Ernie Bragg (Jack Douglas) finds himself a little frosty in parts after a spell in the freezer.

Left: Windsor Davies, one of the caravanners, chats up two of the girls at the camp site.

Above: Professors Vrooshka and Crump (Elke Sommer and Kenneth Williams) digging in harmony at last.

In the scene between Bernard Bresslaw and the mynah bird in **Carry On Behind**, the bird declined to talk. Gerald Thomas came to the rescue, using his own voice for 'Hello darling. Get stuffed. Show us your knickers.' Gerald also provided some of the noises for **Screaming**.

Carry On England

Sergeant Willing (Judy Geeson) and Private Sharp (Joan Sims) eagerly await the tunnellers from the men's hut.

England's air defences in 1940 depend on a shambling shower of men and women in an experimental mixed battery who would rather make love than war.

Eighteen years and 27 films after *Carry On Sergeant* the series went back to the barracks with the same kind of 'up yours' attitude to officers but a new approach to sex. In the good old Carry On days sex was something to giggle and gag about. By 1976 it had become something to do – and the men and women of the anti-aircraft battery are doing it most of the time.

When Major S Melly is posted to the camp as CO he is determined to keep the men and women apart. But they have other ideas. Trip wires, cesspits, soap that colours the skin and a uniform which falls to pieces on a route march are just some of the ordeals to which the pompous little new-broom Major is subjected by the other ranks in their determination to stick to doing what comes naturally.

The Major's final get-tough tactic – the erection of an impenetrable barbed-wire 'chastity fence' between the men's and women's huts – leads to the film's most inventive gag. The men dig a tunnel from their hut to the women's. The women dig one to the men's. At night, they crawl towards each other's huts in their separate tunnels, miss each other, crawl back and miss each other again. The men, having twigged what has happened, decide to stay put and wait for their partners to arrive. The women do the same. Come the dawn, they are still waiting.

Kenneth Connor as the Major and Joan Sims in a throwaway role as a love-lorn private, were the only members of the cast who had been carrying on virtually from the beginning. Windsor Davies, as the Sergeant-Major, frustrated by the presence of women and unable to give tongue to his traditional vocabulary, was a recent recruit to the team, and fresh blood was provided by Patrick Mower and Judy Geeson as the romantically attached gunners Willing and Able, Melvyn Hayes as Gunner Shorthouse and a bevy of bit-part players.

On the production side, there was a new script-writing team, a new editor and a new musical director succeeding Eric Rogers, who had provided the music for 21 of the previous Carry Ons.

Sergeant Bloomer (Windsor Davies) inspects the troops. A more motley crew could not be found.

Kenneth Connor	Captain S. Melly
Windsor Davies	Sergeant Major 'Tiger' Bloomer
Patrick Mower	Sergeant Len Able
Judy Geeson	Sergeant Tilly Willing
Jack Douglas	Bombardier Ready
Diane Langton	Private Alice Easy
Melvyn Hayes	Gunner Shorthouse
Joan Sims	Private ffoukes Sharpe
Peter Jones	Brigadier
Peter Butterworth	Major Carstairs

Also starred:

David Lodge, Julian Holloway, Linda Hooks, Patricia Franklin, Vivienne Johnson, Barbara Rosenblat, Johnny Briggs, Brian Osborne, Larry Dann and Jeremy Connor.

Producer	Peter Rogers
Director	Gerald Thomas
Screenplay	Jack Seddon and David Pursall
Cinematographer	Ernest Steward RSC
Music	Max Harris
Editor	Richard Marden

89 min. Colour. 1976. Cert. AA.

Right: what is Emmannuelle (Suzanne Danielle) doing to her dinner guests beneath the table? Wouldn't you like to know?

Suzanne Danielle	Emmannuelle Prevert
Kenneth Williams	Emile Prevert
Kenneth Connor	Leyland
Jack Douglas	Lyons
Joan Sims	Mrs Dangle
Peter Butterworth	Richmond
Larry Dann	Theodore Valentine
Beryl Reid	Mrs Valentine

Also starred:

Henry McGee, Howard Nelson, Stanley McGeach, Claire Davenport, Norman Mitchell, Albert Moses, Tricia Newby, Tim Brinton, Corbet Woodall, Robert Dorning, Bruce Boa, Michael Nightingale, Eric Barker, Malcolm Johns, Jack Lynn, Guy Ward and Victor Maddern.

Producer	Peter Rogers
Director	Gerald Thomas
Screenplay	Lance Peters
Music	Eric Rogers
Cinematographer	Alan Hume RSC
Editor	Peter Boita

88 min. Technicolor. 1978. Cert. AA.

Carry On Emmannuelle

The lovely Emmannuelle Prevert seduces the butler, the chauffeur, the Prime Minister, the Commissioner of Police, a High Court Judge, the American Ambassador, an Arab diplomat, an Admiral and an entire football team but fails to get her husband, Emile, into bed with her until the final reel.

'Why me?' cries Emile Prevert, the French Ambassador to England, who has become temporarily impotent after a close encounter with a church steeple while hang gliding. 'Why me?' he asks his wife. 'You can have Tom, Dick and Harry'. 'But I don't want Tom and Harry', replies the ravishing Emmannuelle. She has been busily ravishing almost every male in view, from the ageing Embassy retainers to the distinguished guests at a top-level diplomatic dinner.

Emmannuelle's first conquest, Theodore Valentine (Larry Dann), whom she seduces in the toilet-cabin of a London-bound Concorde, falls madly in love with her (his mother – Beryl Reid in her only Carry On – tells him, 'You're just like your father. He went after a slip of a girl without my permission, too'.)

Despairing of Emmannuelle's casual attitude towards him, Theodore leaks the names of all her distinguished conquests to the press and creates a national sensation. In a live TV interview she turns the tables on the presenter Harold Hump (Henry McGee) by seducing him in front of the watching millions.

As Emmannuelle, long-legged newcomer Suzanne Danielle sails through the action in stylish manner and very few clothes. Kenneth Williams, as Emil, spends much of his time in boxer shorts exercising his puny body and resisting her advances. His bottom gets a great deal more exposure than does his wife's bosom, which is revealed in discreet glimpses.

Other Carry On veterans play the sex-mad Embassy retainers – the housekeeper Mrs Dangle (Joan Sims), the chauffeur Leyland (Kenneth Connor), the butler Lyons (Jack Douglas) and the elderly bootboy Richmond (Peter Butterworth). Gathering below stairs, they recall their most bizarre sex experiences. The best of the flashbacks is Mrs Dangle's rose-tinted memory of a brief encounter with a man (Victor Maddern) in a crowded laundrette – an erotic slow-motion fantasy of underwear and suds.

In all the previous films, the players had been nudging and hinting about sex, chasing and backing away from it and gagging and punning about it, but never actually doing it. With a change of scriptwriter – and a change of moral climate in the late Seventies – the mixed unit of gunners in *Carry On England* appeared to be getting down to it. In *Carry On Emmannuelle* the naughty subject is at last tackled head on.

Index

Carry On films are listed under the second part of their title, e.g. *Sergeant, Nurse* etc. Page numbers in *italic* refer to the illustrations.

PHOTOGRAPHIC ACKNOWLEDGEMENTS

Stills from the films *Carry on Sergeant, Nurse, Teacher, Constable, Regardless, Cruising, Cabby, Jack, Spying, Cleo, Cowboy* and *Screaming* are published by courtesy of Weintraub Screen Entertainment; stills from the films *Don't Lose Your Head, Follow That Camel, Doctor, Up The Khyber, Camping, Again Doctor, Up The Jungle, Loving, Henry, At Your Convenience, Matron, Abroad, Girls, Dick, Behind, England,* and *Emmannuelle* are published by courtesy of The Rank Organisation plc.

CARRY ON VIDEOS

The following Carry On films can be obtained on video from:

Warner Home Video/Weintraub Screen Entertainment		*The Rank Organisation plc*	
Carry On Sergeant	Carry On Spying	Carry On . . . Don't Lose Your Head	Carry On Henry
Carry On Nurse	Carry On Cleo	Carry On . . . Follow That Camel	Carry On At Your Convenience
Carry On Teacher	Carry On Cowboy	Carry On Doctor	Carry On Abroad
Carry On Constable	Carry On Screaming	Carry On Up The Khyber	Carry On Matron
Carry On Regardless		Carry On Camping	Carry On Girls
Carry On Cruising		Carry On Again Doctor	Carry On Dick
Carry On Cabby		Carry On Up The Jungle	Carry On Behind
Carry On Jack		Carry On Loving	Carry On England